High on Business

The Life, Times, and Lessons of a Serial Entrepreneur

by Alan Newman
with Stephen Morris

Foreword by Ben Cohen
Afterword by Jerry Greenfield

Hey ... Help Me Out!

This is the page where traditional publishers print "Advance Praise" from other famous authors and Hollywood celebrities. Three problems:

1. This is not a traditional book.

2. I don't know any famous authors.

3. I don't know any Hollywood celebrities.

So I'm counting on you to help me out. Tell me what you think of my book. Either email me directly at Alan@AlchemyandScience.com or post a review on Amazon.com.

Be honest. While I'm as vulnerable to flattery as anyone else, honest reactions are much more interesting than flowery statements of extravagant praise. Well, praise is nice, too, just don't go overboard. Future editions of this book will feature reader comments and reviews on this page.

My job as a writer is done. Now I can return to the task of getting "high" on that next "fix" that comes only from the adrenaline rush of business.

Alan Newman

High on Business

The Life, Times, and Lessons of a Serial Entrepreneur

by Alan Newman

with Stephen Morris

Parts of this story have been published previously in *Inc.* magazine (November 1, 2004; "It's Not Easy Being Green" by Jess McCuan) and *Vermont Business* Magazine (November 1, 2006; "Vermont's Serial Entrepreneur" by Joyce Marcel.)

cover photo: Michael Metz
back cover photo: Anne Rothwell
editing: Stephen Morris and Stephen Robert Frankel
book and cover design: Michael Potts

What would a book be without the proverbial *Thank yous*? So mine are:

Thanks, Mom—you were my greatest fan and always encouraged me, even though I lived on a different planet than yours.

Thanks to my family—Zak, Zoe, Judy & Julie—for your tolerance and support over the years.

And last, but not least, thanks to all the stakeholders—investors, employees, and other partners who have been willing to work with me and help bring my "paintings" to life. You were (mostly) overworked, underpaid, and a joy to work with. None of this would have happened without you.

Thank you all.

It Takes One to Know One
Foreword by Ben Cohen

Like Alan Newman, I'm trying to figure out what to do for my next act.

I still work with Ben & Jerry's on issues of social activism. I feel good about the fact that the company is shifting its purchasing policies to put more emphasis on buying Fair Trade products. Fair Trade, in which the payment of a higher price to producers in developing countries who adopt higher social and environmental standards, is one of those ideas that has been around for years. When the principles of Fair Trade finally take hold with a huge organization like Unilever (who now own Ben & Jerry's), perhaps something meaningful is happening.

I feel good that a lot of large companies are doing social audits, even if some of them are using it more as a self-congratulatory marketing tool than a bold and honest look at themselves in the mirror. Others are doing it quite well and proving the concept that profitability and social responsibility go hand in hand. Having loyal and enthusiastic customers gives a company a competitive advantage.

Businesses are definitely conducting themselves better now. No doubt about it, and it's because customers are demanding it. More and more companies are understanding that connecting with customers based on shared values is good business.

Now, if we could get the Federal government to grasp this same concept—but don't get me started on the national debt and the 800-pound gorilla in the room, military spending.

I miss the raw adrenaline rush of being part of a growing business that is both successful financially and finding new ways to leverage its power to address social needs. I miss the stimulation of being in a room full of people who are debating whether some idea or policy is consistent with the brand. I miss coming up with the flavors that have a social benefit.

I'm not much of a beer drinker, but I could tell that Alan Newman was doing a beautiful job of building a brand at Magic Hat. And he's one of the few people who has been able to bring branding magic to more than one situation.

Alan is a creative, fun-loving, hard-working guy who is a master when it comes to building a brand. He's also a perfectionist who pays attention to the tiniest details that reflect on the image of the brand. You see it in the product names, the packaging, the events, even the sculptural tap knobs that set Magic Hat apart from the rest of the brewing pack. Everything that the consumer sees reflects not only on the company, but on Alan personally.

At the same time, he's a fearless problem-solver who understands that entrepreneurs face obstacles on a daily basis. They have to find ways around or through all kinds of situations for which they have no background or training. They have to keep things going. I know this because Alan and I have swapped war stories. It's as true for us as for all other entrepreneurs. I guess it takes one to know one.

When Jerry and I started making ice cream, our goal

was to sell the company after a few years and to go off and become . . . I don't know—truck drivers or something. The last thing we wanted to become were "businessmen," because as all old hippies know, business is evil. But something unexpected happened along the way. We morphed into actually being the business. It's a bit hard to explain, because it's a relationship that in some ways goes beyond marriage.

So, we were the business and business was evil— what to do? We decided to see if it was possible to use our business as a force for progressive social change: to integrate a concern for the community into as many day-to-day business activities as possible.

And we decided to do something really weird— honest marketing. All our competitors were positioning themselves as sophisticated European brands. (Do you really think Häagen-Dazs comes from Holland?)

We decided to be unsophisticated.

Our competitors were pretentious; we decided to be unpretentious. Our competitors were pseudo-Europeans; we were two guys from Vermont.

We even put our fuzzy faces on the package so you could see who you were buying ice cream from. We did everything possible to inject our personalities into the brand. In terms of marketing, we turned away from traditional print advertising in favor of events where you could actually get people to put the product in their mouth. I smiled when I read this described as "not high-tech marketing, but high-touch." For sure, I've given away a lot of ice cream in my life.

The demands of running a growing business can take a toll on lives, health, relationships, and marriages, and Jerry and I are fortunate that our own friendship has withstood all these tests. We were friends before we were partners. We came from the same place and we had the same goals—to become truck drivers, remember?

Once this entrepreneur thing gets into your blood, it's impossible to get it out. All the comfort, leisure time, and ego strokes in the world can't replace it. I'm glad to see other businesses learning from Ben & Jerry's. I'm glad to see big companies doing social audits. I'm glad that we've re-directed the course of business at least a little. But there's a certain itch that can only be scratched by creating something from nothing, from going where no one else has gone.

Alan Newman understands this, and I can't wait to see what he does next. Maybe I'll give him a call.

*— **Ben Cohen***

Ben Cohen is the "Ben" of Ben & Jerry's.

Introduction
High on Business
or the Fire Walker and Mom's Theory of More-So

*Hello, my name is Alan, and I have to admit that — I — am — a — serial entrepreneur, hopelessly addicted to business and endlessly in search of my next adrenalin rush. There, I've said it. But I'm also an artist. I paint "pictures" (called businesses) first in my head, then on the canvas called life. Moreover, in the words of the **Wall Street Journal**, I am a "serial entrepreneur," which at least sounds a little more respectable than a "psychopathic opportunity seeker."*

If this sounds ominous, as if I'm an alcoholic, dope fiend, or seriously ill, then I've hit the right note, because to be an entrepreneur is to set out on a journey that is sure to be marked by ecstatic highs, gut-wrenching lows, a million blind alleys, strained relationships, and uncertainty. If you want an advanced degree in navigating uncharted waters, start a business.

On the positive side, you will rarely be bored.

As I write this, I am in New Orleans, my current winter home. It's the Saturday before "Fat Tuesday," the day of the Mardi Gras parade that we started in Burlington, Vermont seventeen years ago.

It's sunny here, in the sixties (just like me!). The daffodils are up. I just checked the Burlington weather on my iPhone. Rain is predicted for Burlington. Not the ideal forecast, but like I say, nothing can dampen this event. When winter-crazed Vermonters decide to have a good time, they're not about to be deterred by nasty weather. The parade has happened in sub-zero weather, snow, rain—you name it. Everything but warm and balmy, which is what we have in N'awlins today.

I love N'awlins, because it has it's own culture. I see it in the food, in the music, and especially in the people. I lived in the Marigny neighborhood, and at the end of a few weeks, I knew everyone and everyone knew me.

This is a great place to be. My days are filled, but I'm not sure exactly with what. Life, I guess. This is a little hard to believe, but at an age when I should be handed the gold watch, I'm looking into buying another business. I suppose I could retire. I tell people I can't afford it, but the truth is I'm a junkie, high on business.

The business I'm looking at is in the beverage industry, so it taps into my experience with Magic Hat. The current owner has too much going on and doesn't really have time to run another business. It would take me less than a year to get things really humming. We've toyed with the idea of becoming partners, but I rejected that prospect. I could live with him in a minority role, so that he would have a stake in the company's success down the road. But, at this stage of my life, it will have to be my sandbox.

There are so many unknowns in business, and any one of them can do you in. Is the business as represented? Will the market hold? Will another Katrina hit? One lesson I've learned is how to deal with fear of the unknown. Fear is one of the most powerful human emotions, and its most usual effect is to invoke paralysis. Years ago, I attended a conference which dealt with this and taught us to harness the power of fear and to turn it into positive and productive energy. At the culmination of the session, the leader took us outside to where a hot bed of glowing coals was awaiting. He told us to walk across the coals in our bare feet. I said, "Are you crazy? Those suckers are hot! My feet will be charred flesh by the fifth step." The leader responded, "Don't worry about the fifth step. The only one you need to worry about is the first." I walked across those coals. So did others. Not everyone did, however.

I have walked across those coals countless times in my business career. It's what being an entrepreneur is all about. I won't pretend that it never gets a little warm for comfort, but I will say that I've always reached the other side.

I don't know if this deal will happen. If I'm going to buy this business, I have to buy it right, and I'm not sure the current owner is really ready to let it go. Meanwhile, it's warm and sunny. There's a buzz in the air that is more than springtime. In a few hours this town will be rolling, with great music everywhere.

Another thing that's happening at the moment is that I'm talking with some venture capital people who are interested in buying a Vermont company, have me run it for a few years solidifying the brand, then possibly offering it to the public as the centerpiece in a stock offering. Venture capital likes to invest in people more than bricks and mortar, especially people with a track record. They know that the marketplace is riddled with uncertainty, and they want people who have proven that they can adapt to changing conditions.

If nothing else, I've demonstrated resiliency over the years. The only fly in this ointment is that there is no company to buy at this moment. Something will turn up. It always does. That's a lesson I learned from my father, who was a developer of shopping malls on Long Island. He'd work hard for a year getting a mall up and running, then he'd take a year or two off. He never seemed to worry about where the next meal or paycheck was coming from, so why should I?

Here's the plan for Tuesday, when this town will go crazy. My girlfriend Julie and I will hit the road by 8 a.m. First, we'll catch the Zulu parade a few blocks from our apartment, then we'll get on my current vehicle of choice, a Vespa scooter, and head off to catch some of the Indian activities and parades. Mardi Gras is much more than a big party on Bourbon Street. It's about the fabulous patchwork of cultures and ethnicities that make up this community.

A side note on cars. You'll hear my entire vehicular history in this book. I love to drive. I love the feeling of being in control. Driving is as close as I get to religion. I own a BMW (330 convertible—which I sold an '08 M3 to get—go figure) and a Kawasaki Nomad motorcycle, but here in the city, the Vespa is perfect. We even take it in the rain. You can get anywhere faster than a car, and it solves the parking problem, too.

After the traditional Indian parades, we'll meet a friend for a late lunch. Then, there are a couple of bands I'd like to hear. There's music non-stop in this town, especially at this time of year. We'll be home by 6 or 7 p.m. Do a round of e-mails, see if the day has brought any surprises, pack the car so we can get out early the next morning, then call it a night.

One of my supposed friends once described me as having "the attention span of a gnat," and I suppose it's true. Give me one single thing to do, and it will probably never get done. Give me six or seven balls to juggle, however, and I'm in my element.

My Mother had a theory about this, her "More-So" theory: We all have quirks of personality, and as we get older, we still retain whatever quirks we had when we were younger ("younger" being a relative term that I continually redefine), only these quirks get "more-so." In my observation and experience this has proved 100 percent true.

On the surface, it might seem like I'm taking a break from being an entrepreneur. But here in New Orleans, I have spring weather, Julie, the Indian parades, old friends, great music, and my trusty iPhone to keep me plugged in. Sounds like a pretty perfect day to me. I'm the same guy I was when I was riding my bike delivering papers on Long Island, or getting stoned listening to Big Brother and the Holding Company on Mt. Tamalpais, or leading the Burlington Mardi Gras parade with the mayor of the city.

The same guy, only more-so.

I don't consider myself exceptionally smart, certainly not a business genius. But I have experienced a lot in a wide variety of businesses, and I've made my share of mistakes. If I can help a fledgling entrepreneur not bang his or her head against the same brick wall as I have—if I can stop you from pissing on your own shoes—then I will have accomplished what I set out to do.

When I set out to write this book, the first thing I did was to realize that I don't know anything about writing a book. I did what I always do and contacted someone who knows a lot more about books than I do: Stephen Morris. My career has intersected with Stephen's at various points over the past thirty years. He was at Vermont Castings when I was with National Gardening and Gardener's Supply, at Real Goods when I was at Seventh Generation, and at Chelsea Green Publishing while I was at Magic Hat. He's even written a book about beer! His book **The Great Beer Trek** influenced a number of the early pioneers in the craft beer business.

This book was created via iPhone and e-mail, with lots of help from my friends. Thanks y'all.

Mardi Gras in Vermont

from the memory banks of Stacey Steinmetz, Director of Marketing, Magic Hat Brewing Co.

Magic Hat was looking for a means to give back to our downtown customers after executing a large-scale Halloween event at our brewery. Apparently, we had, unwittingly, usurped all Halloween party-goers, leaving the bars and restaurants sparse on what should have been one of their best nights of the year. Not a terribly bright move for the new start-up brewery.

I was traveling to Florida, and it dawned on me that the Mardi Gras celebration I attended in the funky area of Soulard County in St. Louis would be a fabulous Magic Hat community event. The event could not have been any more defined in my mind, and I excitedly called Alan to share with him my idea and the mechanics of how it would work:

"I'll get all my bars and restaurants to do floats, a participation fee will cover the cost of beads and a donation to a non-profit, we'll get the community radio and newspaper to promote the event, we'll have a local band play after the parade, and it will all benefit a community non-profit who will, in turn, help us secure volunteers to pull this thing off. Everyone will come out to support it, the bars and restaurants will get a "'new'" holiday and the non-profit will gain awareness through PSA's and event promotion and a small donation through participation fees. It's a win-win idea!"

"That's the stupidest thing I ever heard," was Alan's blunt response when I finally stopped my exuberant explanation to catch my breath. "You realize we are talking the middle of winter in Vermont."

Having gone to college at the University of Vermont, I instinctively retorted, "If you give people a reason to party, they will." In Alan's typical, flippant manner, he encouraged me onward with: "Stacey, have a ball."

About 1,500 people came to the event that first year. Now the parade routinely brings 25,000 people to downtown Burlington and more than $130,000 has been raised in support of the Women's Rape Crisis Center.

Appendix

Why is an appendix called an appendix? An appendix is a narrow tube protruding from the cecum, having no known useful function. (Do you even know where your "cecum" is?)

So why is the same word in the English language used to describe the extra material that appears at the end of a book? Does it serve no useful purpose? And why is the plural "appendices?"

It makes no sense, so I'm putting the appendix of this book here at the beginning. Who makes these rules, anyway?

Another rule is that stories have a beginning, middle, and end. Why? That's not the way I want to tell this story. So I think it will be helpful to have a chronology and a cast of characters where it will be most useful. Right here:

Chronology

1906 My maternal grandparents emigrate to Brooklyn from Poland.

1912 My paternal grandparents emigrate to Brooklyn from England.

1945 My parents marry.

1946 November 10: At least 1,400 people are killed in an earthquake measuring 7.4 on the Richter Scale, in the Ancash Region and Quiches District in Peru.

The Slimbridge Wetland Reserve opens in England.

Alan Newman is born in Brooklyn, New York.

1949 The Newman family moves to Long Island.

1955 The Dodgers win the World Series, beating the Bronx Bombers.

1956 I get my first paper route.
Dodgers lose to Yanks in World Series.

1957 Dodgers play final game at Ebbets Field before moving to L.A.

1965 I graduate from high school (barely).
I finally get my gas-guzzling 1958 Corvette

1966 Extended visit to Haight-Ashbury. I become a hippie.

1967 Summer job at the Hilltop Inn.

1969 December 1: first Draft Lottery is held. November 10 comes through big-time. I'm safe!

1970 I graduate from college.
My first move to Vermont.

1971–73 The KaramelKorn era in Fall River, Massachusetts.

1972 My son Zak is born.

1975 Back to Vermont.
I move to Hanksville, Vermont, and get a job with University Health Center.

1976 Rural Health Centers Consulting.

1979 Yacht time-share fiasco with Tony.

1981 Hired by Gardens For All as "the computer guy."

1982 I follow Will Raap to Gardener's Supply Company.

1984–87 Transition to Niche Marketing.

1988 Change ReNew America catalog to Seventh Generation.

1989 My daughter Zoe is born.

1989 I meet Jeffrey Hollender. We become equal partners.

1991 My six-month sabbatical from Seventh Generation gets extended.

1993 I found Magic Hat with Bob Johnson.

We sponsor our first Blues Festival.

1994 Flynn St. Brewery opens.
Stacey Steinmetz becomes our first employee.
First packaged beer from Shipyard arrives.

1995 Mike Brown joins Magic Hat.

1997 Bartlett Bay Brewery opens with money loaned by Key Bank.
Steve Hood joins Magic Hat.

1998 Key Bank calls loan.
Partnership with Todd Enright.

2004 Martin Kelley joins Magic Hat, then IBU.

2007 Financial partnership with Basso Capital Management L.P.

2008 Pyramid deal.

2010 August 11: I leave Magic Hat for good.
I found Alchemy and Science Industries.

2011 Publish my book!

Cast of Characters

Ross Anderson	Friend, financial adviser, and investor in Magic Hat
Ben Cohen	Legendary ice-cream maker and social innovator
Todd Enright	Venture capitalist.; Investor in Magic Hat and key advisor.
Greg Gatta	Liaison with Basso Capital Management L.P., investment firm
Jerry Greenfield	Another legendary ice-cream maker and entrepreneur
Jeff Hollender	Partner in Seventh Generation
Steve Hood	Operations manager at Seventh Generation, and later at Magic Hat
Bob Johnson	Brewer, baker, chef, and co-founder of Magic Hat
Martin Kelley	President of Magic Hat
Arnie Koss	Co-founder of Earth's Best
Hinda Miller	Co-founder of Jogbra
Judy Newman	My ex-wife
Will Raap	Founder of Gardener's Supply Company
Jack Robinson	President of Gardens For All
Stacey Steinmetz	First employee of Magic Hat
Lyman Wood	Founder of Garden Way and a million other companies
Matt Zambarano	Early brewer at Flynn Ave. Brewery

22 : Alan Newman

Chapter 1
The Wrong Question ...

Over the years, many people have asked me "How do you get into a business?" This is the wrong question. Getting into business takes about fifteen minutes and a couple hundred dollars. The question no one asks, and the part of the equation I've never done well with is "Once you've started a business, how do you get out of it? Here's a story to tell you how not-to do it. I call it "The Beginning of the End, or ... End of the Beginning?"

Lesson: The Drag-along Clause

You don't sign a drag-along clause because you want to. You don't sign a drag-along clause because you're smart or it makes sense. You don't sign a drag-along clause because you don't understand it. You sign a drag-along clause, because the person you are dealing with—most likely your financial partner—has a gun, and it is pointed at your head.

A drag-along clause, sometimes called a bring-along provision, forces a shareholder to sell his/her shares in a company if a certain threshold of stockholders and/or the board of directors approve the transaction. Hence the term, "drag-along."

In June, 2010 I learned that my financial partner sold his majority share of Magic Hat Brewing Company, which I had started in 1994, to the one company I had requested we not be sold to. Because I had signed a drag-along requiring me to sell at the same price as my financial partner, I was forced to go along. I was never even given the specifics of the deal until it closed—that's how relevant I was. Kind of like being a ghost in the company I started.

An entrepreneur starts businesses, but he should know how to end them as well. The word is of French origin, a combination of *entre* ("between") and the verb *prendre* ("to take"). The entrepreneur takes an enterprise, idea, or venture and takes possession of it. He is the person between capital and labor. He has full responsibility for the outcome. With Magic Hat, I am as responsible for the outcome as the origin. But Magic Hat clearly didn't end up where I wanted—with me out of a job and with the company in the hands of someone else. There's a lesson here.

Magic Hat started on the proverbial shoestring in November, 1994. My brewing buddy, Bob Johnson, and I opened our small, draft-only brewery in Burlington. Simultaneously, our first bottled six-packs started coming in from Maine, produced for us by another brewery.

We were low to the ground, grass-roots. I put up the early money and started juggling credit cards. I convinced a few friends to invest. We were profitable and cash-flow positive from the getgo (with no salary for me, and Bob at a very low salary). We got a small SBA-guaranteed loan. Bob and I could do what we wanted. In case of disagreement, I had the final say. It was very clear.

Sales took off; we were a hit from day one. As the Kinks say in *Top of the Pops*, "Life is easy when your record's hot." We sold every barrel of beer we could brew. We added storage tanks. We hired people. We expanded to two shifts. We ran out of space to add capacity. Damn. That sure was quick. It's 1996.

What happens to these plucky lads? How do they turn surefire success into ignominious purgatory? Why does Bob wind up running a bakery in Maine? Who gets the money? And why is Alan sitting on his ass in N'awlins writing a book? You'll just have to keep reading. For me the movie is over. It's time for a new movie.

The bullet that was fired by Key Bank in September 1997 (when it lent us a bunch of money) finally resulted in death on August 11th, 2010, but who's counting? Once again, I had proved more adept in starting up a company than in creating a personal exit strategy.

Lesson: My Grandfather and Valentine's Day

I have "emigrated" from Long Island to Vermont. Not exactly a big deal in today's mobile society. I'm only two generations removed from grandparents who were true immigrants, leaving their roots in Eastern Europe and England, respectively, to come to Brooklyn, passing through Ellis Island in the years before World War I and settling in an enclave of people like themselves.

My maternal grandfather adapted very easily to his new country and became a very successful jobber, or what today we would call a wholesaler—successful, that is, until the market crash of 1929. It wasn't so much that he owned a bunch of suddenly worthless stocks, but rather that he was stuck with a warehouse full of chocolates at a time when luxury items were the first thing cut from people's shopping lists. So he figured a way around this problem by exploiting the circumstance in which he found himself: The family legend is that another jobber in the same warehouse was stuck with an over-supply of red, heart-shaped boxes. My grandfather put the chocolates in boxes just in time for Valentine's Day in 1930, and the rest, so the cliché goes, is history.

I don't claim that my grandfather invented Valentine's Day or even that he was the first person to think of putting chocolates into heart-shaped boxes; but there is certainly a lesson here that has stayed with me throughout my business career. Adversity can create great opportunity, especially when you have nothing to lose.

You like Buffalo Wings, the perfect accompaniment to beer? The story is that they were invented at the Anchor Lounge in Buffalo, New York when the Friday night meat delivery was screwed up and consisted entirely of chicken wings. Rather than bemoan their fate, the owners hailed it as the start of a new Friday night tradition.

At Starbucks, they toss a pot of coffee after 30 minutes and replace it with fresh. Sure it wastes coffee, but a customer never has to be concerned with getting a stale cup of coffee. It's a small but integral part of the overall Starbucks experience. That's how you build brand loyalty.

My writing collaborator Stephen Morris tells a story about his early days at Vermont Castings when the company was one of hundreds of wood stove companies operating across the U.S. What made Vermont Castings unique was that they were selling their 450-pound stoves direct to the consumer. He was customer service manager when the stoves started to malfunction due to a catastrophic failure of an internal part. Can you imagine the difficulty of handling a service problem with a 450-pound object that has been shipped to California? A failure like this can torpedo a company.

Morris went to the founders of the company, Duncan Syme and Murray Howell, for guidance. They didn't have a solution, but told him "Whatever you do, just make sure it exceeds the customer's expectations." Armed with that instruction, the customer-service staff spent the next couple of years exceeding customer expectations. In the process, Vermont Castings developed one of the most fanatical customer followings ever. The first time they held a customer open house, 3,000 people showed up from all over the country. The next year, 10,000 people came.

There are myriad examples of things going the other way, of once-great brands being tarnished by cover-ups and shortsightedness. Can anyone say "BP?" Maybe it really does stand for "Burn the Planet." Toyota's impeccable reputation for quality took a huge hit when they tried to minimize rather than confront their braking problem.

S%#* happens!! Things are sailing along smoothly when the market crashes, the part fails, the wrong item is delivered, someone dies, the hurricane hits, the bank calls the note, and the shit hits the fan. If you're an entrepreneur, you hit the wall, bounce up, dust yourself off, and head for the next opportunity.

Grandpa Joe taught me that.

Life is not a straight line. Who said that? I guess it was me. (My writing partner tells me this correctly should be "I guess it was 'I,' but that doesn't sound like me.") Here's an example of when my life took one of its unexpected turns:

Life: Saved by the Bell

As an entrepreneur, it's your job to be ready for anything. Opportunity does not operate on a fixed schedule.

My last "real" job (meaning that I was an employee of someone else) was when I worked at Gardens for All, a non-profit division of Garden Way. Although it was a non-profit, the organization ran a small mail-order division selling "enabling tools" for gardeners. Overall, this was a good experience that exposed me to another serial entrepreneur (Lyman Wood) and connected me with some fledgling entrepreneurs (Will Raap and Jack Robinson), but after less than a year I was nearing the end of my "working for someone else" tether. Also, I had completed a crash course in basic direct marketing and computers—the reasons I had taken the job to begin with. The learning curve had flattened out, and it was time to move on. But . . . how to tell my boss, Will Raap, who managed the catalog and who had treated me very well?

I puzzled and fretted over how best to give my notice when, on a lovely Friday morning, Will asked if I would go for a ride with him to talk to someone about something down in Southern Vermont. It was irrelevant who we were meeting with or why, but I knew that a long car ride was the perfect setting to work my resignation into the conversation.

But Will was a step ahead of me. Obviously he, too, had an ulterior motive for inviting me on a long car ride. Gardens for All had encountered some threats to its status as a non-profit, due to the fact that it was using its non-profit status to mail catalogs at a reduced rate. The decision had been made to split the operation in two. Jack Robinson, president of Gardens for All, would run the mission-driven non-profit, moving it to more of a magazine subscription-based financial model, while Will would spin off the fledgling mail-order division as a for-profit business selling a broader range of gardening products.

Will asked if I wanted to go along with him in the new company as the vice president, responsible for administration and operations. I tried to stay nonchalant "Interesting . . . Tell me more . . . What else do I have to do? Sign me up!"

A few years later I sold my share of ownership in Gardener's Supply for $200,000, which became my start-up capital for Niche Marketing and Seventh Generation. I can't help but think, however, of how much different things might have been if I had blurted out my resignation before Will had a chance to give me his news.

My life is full of these stories.

Chapter 2
The Gas Station in the Sky

My ex-wife Judy contributes a piece of advice that entrepreneurs routinely ignore. Then, it's up to the gas station in the sky with old friend, Arnie Koss, another entrepreneur with a graduate degree from the school of hard knocks.

I reveal the secret to my marketing success (it has to do with my birthday), and tell one of the most essential skills for the would-be entrepreneur—knowing how to operate a Telex machine.

Lesson: Do the Math

In the immortal words of Judy Newman, my former wife, "Don't get on the road unless you want to go where that road goes." It may seem like Judy has the proverbial "remarkable grasp of the obvious," but I have found there to be considerable wisdom in this statement. It is amazing how many businesses are started that are so conceptually flawed that they never have a chance of success.

Restaurants are notorious for this. Before you spend a million dollars on the renovation and hire the three-star Michelin chef from Paris, PLEASE do the basic math. How many tables? Average number of diners per table? Average ticket (price per meal)? Expected turns (number of times the table will host new diners in a given time period)?

Multiply the variables and you will come up with gross

projected revenues. Now—let me know if this is getting too technical—compare that to your expenses. Here's the key question. Is there any money left over?

I have been amazed at the many instances I have seen where this simple calculation is never done. People fall in love with an idea; they become intoxicated with their own enthusiasm; and before long, customers are flying in and out. Eventually, however, reality prevails. This explains why the majority of businesses fail. (I've heard the number is over 90 percent.) There are any number of valid reasons for business failure, but starting the race with a dead horse should not be one of them.

This can be avoided if you plan to succeed, rather than try to avoid failing, and do your math.

There are two types of people in the world: those who want to know exactly where the road goes before getting on it and those who get on the road without any idea where they are heading. The entrepreneur should fall somewhere in-between, but closer to the latter stereotype.

I have two questions when folks ask if they have what it takes to be an entrepreneur. The two questions determine the level of "dumb" a person has, because you need some "dumb" to do this.

Question #1 — Did you have a newspaper route when you were in sixth grade? Maybe because I did, I started noticing a disproportionate number of entrepreneurs who also did. This demonstrates an early desire to spend your leisure time riding around on a bike, in the cold, rain, and snow, so you can claim to be "in business."

Question #2 —Have you heard of the "gas station in the sky?" This is a story told to me years ago by a fellow Vermont entrepreneur named Arnie Koss:

Arnie, along with his identical twin brother, Ron, founded a company called Earth's Best back in the early '90s. Initially, they made organic baby food, figuring there was an untapped market of mothers who wanted baby products that set new standards for healthy, pure, wholesome foods. They were right. Great idea for a business, I thought.

The Kosses' own story is well chronicled in a new book, *The Earth's Best Story: A Bittersweet Tale of Twin Brothers Who Sparked an Organic Revolution* (Chelsea Green, 2010). Ron Koss, as quoted in the publisher's promotional materials, says, "I was essentially forced out of the company that I started with my identical twin brother, Arnie. Hardly a new or unusual outcome in the founders/private capital war."

Arnie's story, as I remember it, is one that entrepreneurs tell about themselves after a beer or two. This one has always stayed with me. (Sorry, Arnie, if it's not exact. Maybe it will get people to buy your book.)

Being an entrepreneur, says Arnie, is like being a pilot. You're on an island and there's a storm coming. If the storm hits while you're on the ground, there's no telling when you might get off the island.

It takes a full tank of gas to reach the mainland. The gas truck is pumping—but the tank is only half full, and there's no place to refuel between here and land.

What to do?

For the entrepreneur, it's a no-brainer: you just take off, and assume you will figure it out along the way. It's all about making things work.

I've always had an exceptional (and irrational) belief that I can make IT work. That's both the great blessing and the curse that comes from arrogance. In addition to "dumb," arrogance is a required attribute for entrepreneurs. If my financial manager comes to me on Monday saying we don't have the money to make payroll on Friday, I'm likely to respond, "So come back to me on Thursday." There's plenty to get done between now and then.

It's always about creation—about solving the problem, being resourceful, and getting IT done. For me, it's never been about making more money. And that's why time and time again the entrepreneurs will eventually lose out to the private equity guys. When the interests of finance and creation come into conflict, the money people win 100 percent of the time. Entrepreneurs are not playing by financial rules.

Sure, occasionally a Bill Gates or Steve Jobs can bridge the gap between creation and management, and there are cases where an entrepreneur's successes are so strong that they cover up managerial weaknesses; but for each of these, there are a hundred Ron and Arnie Kosses and Alan Newmans out there in their airplanes, counting on a tanker to come along for a mid-flight refueling. And completely confident that it will happen.

In case you haven't figured it out by now, entrepreneurs are as much in need of a Twelve Step help program as alcoholics or drug addicts. They can't stop themselves; they can't help themselves; they can't play by other rules. The name of the game is to accommodate the illness by finding a way to take advantage of it, because every once in a while that tanker does come along.

Life: The Twisted Beaver

Could there be anything more unremarkable than my humble origins? Or less interesting? I was born on November 10, 1946. That date is significant for several reasons (wait until you get to the chapter on the first national draft lottery, during the Vietnam war).

First, I am a Scorpio. I don't know if you believe in these

things, but a few words often used to describe Scorpios are resourceful, observant, passionate, dynamic, manipulative, unyielding, and obsessive.

Guilty as charged.

Here's how Scorpios are described on astrology.com: "Scorpios are fiercely independent. They are able to accomplish anything they put their mind to and they won't give up. They are perfectly suited to being on their own. They are not social butterflies like some other zodiac signs, and some actually prefer to live on their own that way. There is never any issue of who controls what at home; they like to be in control.

"Relationships with Scorpio are always complicated, just like the person; their relationships are a series of extremes, they can even be downright moody for no apparent reason. Scorpios are known for their possessiveness and jealousy, but on the other hand, they are extremely loyal. Scorpios have an excellent memory and combined with an inability to let things go, they can hold a grudge against someone who did them harm forever; in fact, a Scorpio rarely if never forgives and forgets. They will even go as far as get vengeance on the person."

And don't you forget it!

More important than the astrological implications, however, is that 1946 places me at the leading edge of the first wave of the post – World War II Baby Boomers. My father, the dutiful soldier, returned home, like millions of other dutiful soldiers, and made love to his dutiful wife. Nine months later, in Brooklyn, New York, little Alan popped out, as did, elsewhere, millions of other little Alans and Jennifers and Frankies.

What this means is that there are a lot of PLMs out there – "People Like Me" – all with similar cultural experiences, regardless of political persuasions. When I have a gut reaction to something, I can count on the fact that a lot of other people will have that same gut reaction. If something or someone strikes me as cool, outrageous, offensive, or perceptive, the one thing that I can be confident of is that there are a lot more people who will share my perception.

I don't claim a lot in common with Bill Clinton or George W. Bush, both 1946 babies, but I know that we were all about sixteen when JFK was assassinated; we were graduating from high school just when the Beatles became a hit in the U.S.; we were hard-partying college guys when people started experimenting with weed (some of us even inhaling); we went through the first draft lottery together; and we're all now looking at the same window of mortality. We might be at different points of the social or political spectrum, but if I sat down with George or Bill, we'd have a lot of notes to compare. We've shared the cultural touchstones.

It was a new world that our fathers came home to. The Depression was now a distant memory, replaced by a sense of prosperity, security, and entitlement. We lived the first couple years of my life with my grandparents in Brooklyn, but then, along with millions of others, we moved to the suburbs, in our case, to Long Island.

Baby boomers are still calling all the shots in the culture. Get old? Retire? Die? One thing is for sure: we're not going to go about it the same way our parents did.

Over the years, I've participated in zillions of market-research studies and focus groups. These can be helpful learning experiences, but they can also lead to the wrong conclusions. At the end of the day, I've always relied on "a marketing survey of one—me." A decision has to pass my own gut check and smell test. If it works for me, I know it will work for a lot of other people. After all, we're not called the Me Generation for nothing.

But all stories need a beginning, middle, and end. Here's my beginning:

I grew up on Long Island at a time when Long Island was growing up, literally. The mass exodus to the suburbs had begun and farms were becoming Levittowns at warp speed. The Long Island of my youth, however, was not yet paved. There were still woods and marshes and plenty of room for a kid to ride his bike. We had the requisite nuclear family of one dad, one mom, and two children. My younger brother, Steve, was born in 1949.

In many ways it was *Father Knows Best* meets *Leave It to Beaver*. Our family was comfortable, sometimes borderline prosperous. What I remember was the sense that anything and everything was possible and within reach. We walked to school, and later rode our bikes (from first grade on), without parents ever worrying about our safety. We played baseball in the newly -built parks, rode roller skates and bicycles around traffic-free roads. There were always neighborhood friends to play with. We rode in cars without child restraints, or even seat belts—even sitting on the tops of the rear seats of convertibles—without our parents getting arrested for negligence.

Of course, there's a darker side to this idyllic tableau, but I'll save that for later. Things are not always what they seem. Here's a story that proves that point:

Life: The Tale of the Telex

Life has a way of taking 90-degree twists and turns. It's your job to always be prepared.

Following the unmitigated disaster of my KaramelKorn experience in the early '70s (which I haven't told you about yet), Judy and I returned to Vermont in January, 1975. I needed a job and took one at the newly established University Health Center in Burlington. This lasted for nine months, and then I left to help a friend run a smaller health center. This, in turn, led to a job with the Dartmouth Medical School, where I started gaining a reputation as an expert in billing systems and organization structure for rural health centers. Go figure. Eventually I set up my own consulting practice, specializing in rural medical practices. Essentially, I did clean-up operations for small businesses throughout Vermont, New Hampshire, and northern New York.

This is where I will spare you my extended rant on doctors. As with all generalizations, there are exceptions, but I found doctors, as a group, to be the scourge of the earth. Many were spoiled rotten, as if they were a special, anointed breed. They completely misunderstood my role in helping them deliver better health care by being more efficient. Saving lives? That was the last thing on the agenda. Instead, the questions I got were "How do I make more money?" "How do I get people in and out faster?" "How do I avoid liability?"

The doctors I worked with believed it was my job to make them richer. They may have been highly competent professionals, but the side I was exposed to was money-grubbing, petty, and greedy.

I began developing the same kind of disdain for doctors as I had the KaramelKorn kustomers back at the mall. After a particularly galling time with one of the managing partners in a medical practice in White River Junction, I started looking for a "real" job working for someone else. I loved the lifestyle I had with the consulting business, but I couldn't stand the clientele. Time to move on.

For reasons that I don't fully understand, I've never felt compelled to do the logical thing of finding a new job before leaving the old one. I've worked continuously since I was about ten years old, when I got my first paper route. It was nothing drilled into me by my parents. It was internal. I just worked. I never worried about what comes next. Something always comes along. Always.

What came next, however, surprised even me.

By now it was 1978. I had taken a job as the business

manager for a local company, Associates in Rural Development (ARD), doing international consulting work. The favored (and only) means of immediate international communication in those days was a Telex machine. This was in the pre-fax days, which, for younger readers, was in the pre–e-mail days, and which for even younger readers was in the pre–cell phone days.

We needed to buy a new telex machine, and because I had a smattering of technical knowledge, I was charged with researching which brand to buy. "OK," I responded, "but only on one condition: I will research the machine, but I won't learn how to use it." I knew that once I learned to operate the machine, I would be forever relegated to the role of telex operator. It was agreed that our office manager, Lisa, would be the telex operator. The best laid plans . . .

The machine arrived on a day when Lisa was out sick, and of course we had telexes that had to be sent. Guess who became the de facto telex operator? And who would ever guess where this obscure skill would lead?

Six months later, having left ARD and yet another paying job, I was coaching my son, Zak's Little League team. One of the other dads/coaches helping me was a guy named Tony. I didn't know much about him, other than that he was a very interesting guy who was starting up a business. As we're putting away the bats and balls at the end of practice one night, out of the blue, he says to me "Do you know anyone who knows how to operate a telex machine?" That moment, despite my early forays into KaramelKorn and providing business services for doctors, marked the real start of my entrepreneurial career. And I owe it all to Lisa being sick on the day that ARD's telex machine was delivered!

Lesson: Just Because You Can Fly a Plane Doesn't Mean You can Fly a Business

I showed up at Tony's office to help him send his telex message—and stayed for almost two years, which were certainly among the most interesting two years of my life.

Tony's business was a start-up located on the top of a mountain in Hanksville, Vermont. His plan was to offer time-shares in ocean-going, sailing yachts. It seemed like a reasonable enough idea at the time, but now with the benefit of thirty years hindsight, I have to say "What the hell were we thinking?" Time-share? Ocean-going? Yachts? Vermont? Someone had not taken Marketing 101.

Tony had a fascinating background that included little business experience. He graduated near the top of his class at West Point, and was a Navy fighter pilot with a ton of interesting stories and, unlike me, was very much a buttoned-up straight arrow with a highly developed sense of discipline and a military demeanor. (Exactly how he went to West Point and ended up in the Navy is beyond me, but that's how I remember it.)

He told me hair-raising stories of landing jets on aircraft carriers at night, in higher-than-30-foot seas. It was all instinct, he'd say. He'd attend a pre-combat briefing, and then, while everyone else was scurrying getting pumped up to prepare for the mission, Tony would take a nap. Now, that's the right stuff!

Here's just one of his stories : After his Navy stint he worked selling airplanes and sold a fleet of F-14s to the Shah of Iran. Part of that deal, at the insistence of the Shah, was that Tony come live in Iran to train that country's fledgling pilots how to use of these new toys. That's not an assignment that you want to screw up! When it came to anything airborne, Tony had complete confidence and credibility, which made for many evenings of great stories—but had little relevance to starting a time-share business for ocean-going yachts on a mountain in Vermont.

A benefactor had invested $300,000 with Tony to start a new business. Tony decided that this time-share yacht idea was a huge opportunity. I joined in to help put together a business plan and private placement offering. We had a blast swapping stories and flying around New England in chartered private planes. Eventually, we cobbled together a plan, but, predictably, we ran out of money before we could get the business to "fly."

It was a great learning experience. For the first time, I saw how the skills and experience from one business could transfer to another, and I'm not talking about operating a telex machine. Business planning is basically the same, no matter if you're talking health care services, beer, or mail-ordering environmental products. (One of the things I've learned about myself over the years and various businesses is that I'm a very competent planner.)

The main lesson I took away is to start small and learn your business and industry while your costs are low. When you've got a skyrocketing operation, as we had later at Seventh Generation, it's no time to be in learning mode, although that's how it tends to happen. Another lesson is that businesses can be killed by too much money as well as not enough. It was probably the kiss of death for Tony to have that initial $300,000 nest egg. It provided a false sense of security.

Epilogue: Tony and I parted when the business failed, and we went back to our individual pursuits, with many lessons learned. The only time I ever heard anything more about him was when I saw him on the 11 o'clock news a few months later. He had been arrested using a leased Cessna to smuggle pot from Jamaica (Mon). Eventually, he went to jail for eighteen months. Once again, he had not done his marketing homework.

Tony was one of the smartest, most interesting persons I've ever known. I will never understand why he risked jail time to do something he had absolutely no experience with. He was certainly smart enough to know better. He was a straight-shooter and a straight-arrow guy, not a dope smuggler. He should have known that what he was doing almost inevitably leads to jail.

Chapter 3
The Flip Side of the Truth

I explore the role of astrological signs in business success, along with other key factors such as good timing and dumb luck. There is a rich cultural fabric to my life. I have lived in interesting times.

I share a wealth of lessons, including a prediction of turbulence in the near future for mid-sized craft brewers.

Lesson: Timing Trumps Information

We live, supposedly, in an "information age," and most people in business will tell you that information provides the path to the truth. Information sets us free. I'm here to tell you that information is only part of the picture.

Businesses thrive on information, but information is really about looking to the past and projecting it in a straight line into the "future." But the future, like life, doesn't go in straight lines. Economies collapse, volcanoes erupt, planes crash into skyscrapers, bankers get greedy, and rivers overflow their banks. You can't anticipate events like these.

The banks and investment firms of the world are filled with bright, highly -educated young people whose jobs are focused on providing so-called information, but all of them are missing the point that the future is about life and life is about energy. A chart of life or energy will go in any number of crazy directions, none of which will be a straight line. Remember my car ride with Will Raap?

I was on a motorcycle trip in Maine at the end of June 2010 when I got an e-mail from investment banker Greg Gatta telling me (or summoning me) to get back to Burlington to meet the new owners of Magic Hat. The new owners? Up until that moment I thought WE were the owners of Magic Hat. And by "we" I really meant "me." Hadn't I started the company? Didn't I pour my heart and soul into it for seventeen years?

Uh-oh . . . the drag-along clause.

I had known the company was "in play," meaning for sale. Greg's employer, Basso Capital Management L.P., a hedge fund in Stamford, Connecticut had become our financial partner in 2006 when they were rolling in dough and looking for opportunities with significant upside potential. We presented them with a vision of turning Magic Hat, a very solid regional craft brewer, into a national powerhouse through a strategy known as a "roll-up." We were looking to acquire another brewery, which, two years later, turned out to be a West Coast craft brewer, Pyramid Breweries, for over $25 million.

It seemed like a good idea at the time, because no one knew that the economy was going to tank in 2008. No one knew the stock market would crash. No one knew that financial giants like Lehman Brothers would go belly-up. No one knew that General Motors would become bankrupt. General Motors, for crying out loud! No one knew that the Letter of Intent (LOI) we had from a reputable bank to finance the deal would be pulled after the bank crisis—and AFTER we had completed the purchase.

No information predicted this. This was not in the straight-line preparation.

The popping of the real-estate bubble and the resulting bailout of the nation's largest banks made ownership of a small brewery by a hedge fund instantly seem like a silly and frivolous idea, and so Basso was looking to unload us as quickly as possible. I had only one request: do not sell the company to KPS Capital Partners, a private equity company that was already running their own roll-up scheme under the banner of North American Breweries. Seventeen years of sweat and toil to make Magic Hat a respected and viable entity might be about to go down the drain, but let's at least look for a good fit. Maybe a European brewery looking for a strong foothold in the American craft brewing market.

Anyone but KPS! (Guess how this one turns out.)

Times: The Fabulous Fifties Meet the Screwed-up Sixties

Believe it or not (I don't), there are people who think I am a marketing "genius." I've already revealed the secret of my success: I was born on November 10, 1946. From a marketing perspective, it puts me squarely in the first wave of the post–World War II baby boom. I am hardly alone; *au contraire*, there are a lot of people like me, who share my tastes and perceptions.

Raised in an era of unprecedented peace and prosperity in the 1950s, we turned the so-called establishment on its ear in the 1960s by rejecting or redefining the traditional values that made us so privileged. For us, landing on the moon was only "the first small step," as Neil Armstrong said, in a journey destined to take us beyond the "doors of perception" (thank you, Aldous—and Jim).

A lot of the so-called truths of the '50s later turned out to be myths. Eggs are good for you; then eggs are bad for you; then eggs are good for you, but only the whites; then eggs are bad for you because they come from big dirty farms; then eggs are good for you, but only if they are free-range and organic; then eggs are bad for you, because even the free-range, organic operations are frauds. Store-bought is good; now, store-bought is bad. Beer is yellow and drunk by slobs. Wonder Bread builds strong bodies twelve ways!

Rachael Carson told us the environment was fucked up;

Jerry Rubin and Abbie Hoffman told us not to trust anyone over thirty, while Timothy Leary told us to "tune in, turn on, and turn off." Crosby, Stills, and Nash told us to "love the one you're with," while Dylan assured us we'd be "forever young."

We believed them all. I certainly did.

When Joni Mitchell told us in her song "Woodstock" that we had to get "back to the garden," I took her literally and moved to Vermont (even though, I confess, I've never really gardened). We flogged ourselves into shape in our thirties and rejected the food habits of our parents. So long, Wonder Bread, Budweiser, and Swanson's TV dinners. Hello crusty bread, organic vegetables, and hand-crafted beers.

And baby boomers are still calling all the shots in the culture. Get old? Retire? Die? One thing for sure, we're not going to go about it the same way our parents did.

Life: Beneath the Veneer Is Yet Another Veneer

Everyone has a theory, and everyone believes their theory is "the truth." Be careful about what you believe to be truths, because perception is reality—and everyone's is different. Remember I told you how idyllic growing up on Long Island was in the 1950s, and that my life, superficially, was a sitcom like *Father Knows Best* or *Leave It to Beaver*? The truth is, beneath the surface it was a little more twisted, and there was a darker side to the "reality" of my idyllic boyhood. Recent movies such as *Revolutionary Road* (about suburban life in the 1950s) and the popular TV series *Mad Men* (set in the 1960s) explore that dark terrain beneath the veneer of normalcy and upward mobility.

After the birth of my brother Steve, my mother took to her bed and didn't emerge until a decade later. Today, her depression might be given the label of post-partum depression, but that's supposed to go away after a few weeks or months. Most of the time she couldn't even get out of bed.

Luckily, for the first ten or twelve years of my life, I had the world's greatest dad. First of all, he was my primary caregiver, due to my mother's incapacitation. Second, he had a binge style of working that gave him a lot of time off. And finally, he had a go-anywhere, do-anything spirit that was just perfect for a couple of young boys.

I learned several important lessons from my father, more by example than through actual instruction. He was a commercial mall developer who was paid a decent salary to develop the real estate, plus a commission based on how well he was able to fill the space. He always maximized his commissions, so every two to three years he would collect his bonus and could afford to take a year off, sometimes longer. This instilled in me, rightly or wrongly, the sense that something would always come along to cover expenses. He never seemed to fret about the next meal or next paycheck, confident that something would turn up, and that's how it has been for me, too. In New Age parlance, "the universe shall provide"—a very useful trait for a serial entrepreneur.

He also taught me about timing. If ever there was a good time to be a developer of malls on Long Island, it was the 1950s and '60s. The suburbs were exploding at that time, as people— such as my parents —fled the cities for the 'burbs. They all had new houses to decorate and to fill with appliances, and the general affluence—and the new highways—insured that every family had wheels. Given the choice between being a genius and having good timing, I will take the good timing any day.

Mini-Lesson: Take the Cash

My father was as casual as they came—for the 1950s, that is. He insisted that everyone call him by his first name rather than the traditional "Mr. Newman." Maybe that's where I inherited my sense of style, too, although in my father's case "casual" still meant a sport coat and tie. He was spontaneous, too. Want to go the amusement park? Let's go now. The beach? Hop in the car.

My father's father had also been in real estate during the Roaring Twenties. The practice at the time, I'm told, is that the property developer would usually take a cut in the form of a piece of the ongoing action. My grandfather (not the guy in the chocolate business) took a different path and said, "No, I'll take my cut in cash."

Come the Depression, there were a lot of real-estate people with cuts of worthless deals. My grandfather, however, was sitting on a giant wad of cash. As a result, my father grew up in a stately home with chauffeurs to drive him to his private schools.

Meanwhile: Back to the Fifties

My idyllic 1950s, however, became the troubled '60s. My father gets credit for both. I was accumulating anger and frustration from the love I wasn't getting from my mother, and my father was doing his best to make things right. In my memory, my early years were all about riding bikes, playing ball in the parks, trading baseball cards, playing in the woods, and doing things with my dad.

But then came the '60s, adolescence, Vietnam, drugs, sex, and rock-and-roll. The more I became my own person, the less he was a part of my life. As time went by, my mother became my best friend while my dad became a less and less meaningful part of my life. Who would have guessed?

Lesson: But, Is It "Magic Hat"?"

There can be a happy intersection of the forces of analytical information, dumb luck, financial interests, and intuition. There was a good example of this when Martin Kelley joined Magic Hat.

What's really magic about Magic Hat is not that my tenure with the company ended after seventeen years; it's that it lasted seventeen years to begin with. I didn't come to the business as a beer guy. Frankly, I didn't come to the business as a business guy either, but that's kind of the story of this book.

Not being a beer guy was both a strength and a weakness. From the branding perspective it was a strength. Everyone was doing the "craft beer" thing, so we created our brand identity to be the anti-craft brewery. If everyone else in the industry followed one rule, then you could count on us to head 180 degrees in the opposite direction. If everyone else names their beers after classic styles—India Pale Ale, Oatmeal Stout, Hefeweizen—then we're going to name our beers after things that had meaning to us, such as having blind faith (i.e., in life, not the name of the band, as most people thought). If everyone else's brewery tour takes you through the plant following the brewing process, then our factory tour winds above the floor, telling stories of our history and ending perched out over the brewery.

Matching our odd, eclectic, freewheeling counter-culture style proved problematic when we tried to bring in outside "suits" until Martin Kelley joined the company.

Martin came from a much more traditionally corporate background than the rest of us, and while he could never fully "get" the culture of the brand, he gets very high marks for not trying to fuck it up.

He challenged us to articulate the brand more coherently. Although some of the old guard resisted this, ultimately this proved to be a valuable exercise. Martin wanted the brand to be expressed in three words, which led to substantial debate within the company. The three we finally came up with were "irreverent," "distinctive," and "theatrical."

Now we had a yardstick against which we could measure new ideas, be they for a new draft handle, a new product name, or a label design. Is it irreverent? Is it distinctive? Is it theatrical? We finally had a language that could bridge the gap between the hippie and the corporate.

In all start-up businesses people are overworked and underpaid. One of the best ways you can keep people motivated is by giving them some level of creative input. The downside to this is that everyone develops a slightly different interpretation of what constitutes the company and its brand. By having our three-word mantra we were able to have a touchstone to which we could all return periodically.

Is it irreverent?

Is it distinctive?

Is it theatrical?

Is it Magic Hat?

#9 ... Anatomy of a Fruit Beer

West Coast brewers were always about five years ahead of East Coast brewers when it came to innovation. In the mid-1990s, while the East Coasters were still ensconced in their top-fermented, English ale traditions, the West Coast was flowing with everything from peach nectar to chocolate garlic brews. Fruit-flavored wheat beers were very much the rage, and Bob and I thought we could keep Magic Hat ahead of the pack if we developed a fruit beer.

But there was a problem: I hate fruit beers. And I can't get into selling a product that I don't personally like, so I went to Bob with the challenge, "Give me a fruit beer I can drink." Not an easy task. The category was defined by such products as Strawberry Blond by Pete's Wicked Ale and Sam's Cherry Wheat. Well-made products, but I don't like them. Too sweet.

Let Bob tell us how he solved this problem:

"In most fruit beers the sweetness comes from both the malts used by the brewer and the residual sugar in the fruit. These fruit sugars can make for inconsistent

fermentations and inconsistency in the finished beer. From my background in wine, I wanted to approach this as more of an aromatic experience and create 'nose,' or aroma by using fruit essence, as opposed to the fruit itself.

"The fruit I chose was apricot, in part because I know of only one other brewer (Pyramid) making an apricot beer, and they used the fruit, not the essence. Also, apricot has a very delicate white fruit aroma that I believed would pair nicely with and complement the natural malt aromas, as opposed to darker, more powerful red berry fruits. For me it was about balance and nuance. Not a fruit-flavored beer, per se.

"Next, I got away from using wheat. Other brewers choose wheat, because its lighter character lets the fruity qualities come through. Instead, I based my recipe on a pale ale recipe where the only sweetness came from the malted barley. I kept it lightly hopped in both bitterness and aroma. This way, you would more distinctly notice the aroma of the apricot. And as we kept the bittering hops down, there was also a perceived sweetness from apricot essence that was actually the natural sweetness from the barley malts used. This also allowed for absolute consistency in fermentation and final gravity in the finished beer. Leave it to Magic Hat to do things differently!

"#9 passed the taste test with Alan, and with our other customers, too. Originally this was to be our summer seasonal, but when we tried to tell people that summer was over and so was #9, they told us, in no uncertain terms, 'No &*^%!! Way.'"

The upshot: #9 was here to stay.

Lesson: The Truth

There are a few truths that I hold to be self-evident. Here, presented at random, are a few of them. (Take notes, as there might be a test later on.)

#1 (Courtesy of Bill Russell, but I'm paraphrasing this quote because I've seen so many variations on it.) "You're never as good as you think when you're on top, and you're never as bad as you think, when you're down and out." The Newman variation on this theme is "Don't read your own press clippings, but if you do, don't believe them." In other words, I am the same person while leading companies to great heights as I am when we tanked. Genius? Idiot? Neither? Both?

#2 The theory of chaos over evolution: straight-line projections simply extrapolate the past into the future. A plan is always perfect, as long as nothing changes. But something always changes.

#3 Five-year plans aren't worth the paper they are printed on, or the ink that is used. You can make a reasonably detailed and believable plan for the first year of a plan. Years 2 and 3 tend to be straight-line extensions of year 1, demonstrating whatever outcome the investor wants to see (that's how you get the money). Years 4 and 5 — who knows? Who expected the Arab oil embargo, the Gulf War, the collapse of the Twin Towers, the economic meltdown, the Japanese tsunami? You just can't anticipate these things in the real world. The only thing you can be sure of in straight-line planning is that nothing goes straight.

Corollary of #3—the fund-raising variation. If you are in the fund-raising mode, then you should be familiar with the "hockey-stick effect." In this 5-year plan, Year 1 is a continuation of the money-losing mode you are currently in. Year 2 is still a loser, but not quite as bad. In Year 3 you finally reach break-even and might even make a few bucks. (These years are the blade of the hockey stick.) Then, in Years 4 and 5, profitability kicks in and you start making money hand over fist. This is the shaft of the stick. I've seen companies that actually have growth rates like this, but only because it happened, never because it was planned. I've never seen a case where it was planned and it actually came to be— the way it was planned.

#4 You can't find good employees anymore. Bullshit! Employees are not idiots. Most people want to succeed, and they want you to succeed, too. As a business owner, your job is to create a culture where people want to solve problems. In too many cases that I've seen, the company culture is for the employees to glorify the business founder. This can work for a while, but it's rarely a successful long-term strategy. Great company cultures create great employees, not vice versa. While I frequently get the credit for my business successes, the reality is, it is the staff that makes the business work or not.

#5 Private equity invests in people—not in companies, not in ideas, not in technologies. They especially invest in people who have shown an ability to adjust to changing market conditions, because (you know this by now) the only constant is change. The market is always changing, and the survivors are those who can adapt. Business is Darwinian in that way. (Unfortunately, the corollary is: private equity and venture capital firms only care about their return on investment (ROI), and will sell the entrepreneur down the river at (almost) every opportunity. Money ALWAYS wins.

#6 You learn more from failure than success. That's why I'm writing this book —because I figure I have to be one of the smartest guys on the planet by now.

#7 Rules can be broken, but only when you know the rules.

#8 Ideas are a dime a dozen—it's the execution, stupid. Given the choice between a great idea and mediocre execution, and a mediocre idea and great execution, take the great execution. I'm repeating myself, but for good reason. Given the choice between great execution and great timing, take the great timing. There were a lot of real-estate geniuses when prices were going up in 2004 who don't look so smart today.

#9 Jim Koch of Samuel Adams is probably the smartest guy I've ever met. Seriously.

And here's what Jim Koch says about me:

Koch on Newman

When I first saw a bottle of Magic Hat, I thought "Oh, this is just another of these marketing creations like Rhino Chasers and Bad Frog. Probably a bunch of dentists or fund managers who decided that owning a micro-brewery would give them extra status with their cocktail party companions". Little did I know that Alan Newman was nothing of the sort. He was the real thing. Creative, crazy and competent. So I watched as he overcame a bad distributor choice in Vermont to establish a real presence. Then he took his show on the road. His beer was one of an elite group that transcended its local hero status and appealed to beer drinkers well beyond the shadow of his brewery in Burlington. And a Mardi Gras in Vermont! The guy was clearly someone special. So I made it a point to introduce myself to this unique character.

Alan is just Alan. Of course, I've only known Alan as a friend and a competitor (yes, the two can be the same thing in craft brewing). I imagine he might be frustrating to a money-driven investor in his company worrying every day how he's going to get his money out with a juicy return. To me, Alan was always a delight. Generous with his time and insights, wildly creative and innovative, and a sound businessperson who was always focused on creating real value. I never had a conversation with Alan without learning something about craft beer, business or life. I watched with admiration as he overcame so many obstacles to create one of the very few craft brands that worked as well outside its home market as it did inside. I had stumbled into Sam Adams as much by accident as design but Alan seemed to know what he was doing. And Sam Adams was my one and only business. It was all I knew. Alan had a long and checkered history as an entrepreneur. So his perspective on creating a business was unique and invaluable. He reminded me of the Buddha's wisdom. "Life takes the thoughtful man on a path of many windings."

If Jim says this, and he's the smartest guy in the world, then it must be the truth!

Lesson: Direct Marketing 101

The beer business is very social. I've dealt with staff, distributors, retailers, and drinkers on a daily basis. The sheer volume and diversity of truly wonderful people astounded me. Opinions varied and some people were competitive, but most went out of their way to help each other.

I came to brewing from the direct-response industry, pre-Internet. Without exception, the best customers for any catalog were people who bought from other catalogs. Buyers who like shopping by mail for any product will outperform any other list you can rent, even better than affinity groups who do not shop by mail. The more someone purchases by mail, the better a mail-order customer that person becomes for everyone. This was measured and proven mathematically, monitoring performances by a broad range of list segments. This shared information created a level of company-to-company cooperation that I have never seen before or since.

And the craft beer world is similar. Rather than stealing sales from each other, most craft brewers know that if the category grows, it will build the business for all of us. However, there are differences of opinion about what will contribute to category growth. The category has been growing for at least the last fifteen to twenty years now, albeit from a tiny base. During this time, if your company was not also experiencing double-digit growth, you were screwing up.

But now the situation has changed. While more drinkers are looking for craft beers, and bars have been adding and promoting them, and more grocery and convenience stores are giving them shelf space, and more distributors are adding craft beers to their "book," there are also more craft breweries opening. Moreover, the big buys are adding craft-like specialty products to their roster.

Did you ever expect to see a beer/tomato juice/clam product from Budweiser, the King of Beers. Are they looking to be the King of Clams, too?

The combination of slower growth and more players spells challenging times for the craft beer business ahead. Unlike the direct-response industry, where the results are black and white and highly measurable, in the beer business everything is driven by opinion, and everyone has a lot of them. And the rules governing the business vary substantially according to the size of the business.

A few years ago, there were two trade associations serving small brewers. One focused on home brewers and brewpubs; the other on smaller regionals. The factors that determine success for these two groups are very different.

The home brewers and brewpubs value novelty and diversity. The regionals, however, are driven more by efficiencies and economies of scale. (This is a simplification, of course.)

The trade associations merged a few years ago (something I voted in favor of, by the way), but the result is that there is some confusion about what constitutes a "craft" beer and what constitutes growth of the entire category. Thus, while the number of beers are growing, the number of outlets and distributors are growing—so it's more challenging than ever to build a brand.

.

Chapter 4
The Call

I get "The Call" just when I least expected and most needed it, repeatedly. An entrepreneur, if nothing else, seeks opportunity like a heat-seeking missile. My Magic Hat "call" comes when Bob Johnson and I are scrambling to establish Magic Hat, and some unfinished business with Seventh Generation leads to some badly needed start-up capital.

I think back to the first national draft lottery in 1969, when millions of young American men learned whether they would be cannon fodder or carefree hippies. Good ol' November 10 comes through again.

Lesson: Don't Sign the Lock-up

Old Chinese proverb: "May you live in interesting times." I say: "Opportunity may knock, but sometimes it rings."

I have witnessed the sexual revolution and the "British Invasion." I have fought in the battle of the sexes and the battle of generations. I've seen beer evolve from bland, yellow fizz to the dazzling concoctions of the Magic Hats of the world. I've seen two of my fellow '46ers become President of the United States. I've seen the inventions of the television, the personal computer, and the iPhone. I've seen skyscrapers rise and fall and rise again. Interesting times . . . and more so.

There are only a few times in every life when you get "the call." It can be good news, or bad. It can be a blast from the past or a bolt from the future. It frequently comes when you least expect it, and it changes the course of your life. The phone rings . . . And all I can tell you is that you better be ready.

One of my calls came in early 1994, during an early stage of the Magic Hat start-up. Bob Johnson and I were scrambling like crazy—happy guys—doing the things that have to get done in the beginning of any venture. After two and a half years of pain, bitterness, acrimony, accusations and counter-accusations, uncertainty, and flailing about trying to get my life back on track after the wrenching, brutal, and public separation from Seventh Generation, things finally were headed in a positive direction. A lot of water had gone over the dam or under the bridge—choose your preferred cliché.

The phone rang. I answered. It was Peter Demuth, the lawyer for Seventh Generation. After a few opening pleasantries, he said "We need you to sign a lock-up on your shares."

The intervening years since I had been booted out of Seventh Generation had not been kind to the business. I had enough tentacles into the company to know how bumpy the road had been. The wave of environmental fervor that made us the darlings of direct marketing had cooled dramatically after the start of the Gulf War. Somehow it seemed frivolous to be talking about the fragility of the environment when Saddam Hussein was torching oil wells in Kuwait. The infrastructure we had created to handle our expected growth had to be dismantled. No business can react that quickly to yo-yoing demand. There had been mass layoffs. Morale was in the pits.

Moreover, my ex-partner Jeffrey Hollender had to deal with all those private investors who had given us money—not an enviable task.

"What do you mean, a 'lock-up'?" I asked.

The company had run out of money again. I had heard rumors that the plan was to have a public offering of Seventh Generation stock as a means of raising the necessary funds to continue. It was also a strategy for recouping the investments of the original financial partners.

"Stock" is one of those business concepts that is too broad and variable for the scope of a book like this. Briefly, stock is a currency that expresses the ownership of a business enterprise. When I started Seventh Generation, I owned 100 percent of the stock, but there were no specified number of shares, since I owned all of them, anyway.

Eventually, as I needed to bring money into the company, I created "units" or "shares" of stock that could be sold to private equity investors so that they could understand what percent of the company they were acquiring for their investment. The value of shares in a limited offering like this is best summarized by the phrase "whatever someone will pay for it."

When Jeffrey joined the company, we each retained 23 percent of the shares. The rest were sold to private investors to raise the capital that we needed to grow. Now, the company was planning an IPO (Initial Public Offering) to offer shares to the public. Such offerings are highly regulated by the SEC (Securities and Exchange Commission) and require boatloads of paperwork. All T's must be crossed and I's dotted before such an offering can move forward to the underwriters, the financial-service providers who actually offer the stock for sale.

A lock-up, explained Peter, is a legally binding contract between the underwriters and insiders of a company prohibiting these individuals from selling any shares of stock for a specified period of time, typically 180 days (six months) but as long as 365 days (one year). There are a couple of reasons for this, but the real purpose of a lock-up is to let the market determine the stock price by preventing a multitude of (non-offering) shares from hitting the market and thus, dragging down the value of the stock.

I'm not an expert in these things, but I knew enough to ask the right question: "What if I don't sign?" Peter immediately launched into lawyer-ese, telling me that it was completely routine and in my best interests to sign. At present, my 23 percent was essentially of no value, because private investors were not exactly clamoring to invest in a money-losing venture. If there's a public offering that establishes a value for the stock, then my 23 percent could actually be worth something at the expiration of the lock-up agreement.

Yes, that part I understood, "but what happens if I don't sign the lock-up?"

The answer was, "Nothing."

But "nothing" can mean "something," and in this case it meant a lot of something. Without my signature on the lock-up, the public offering could not move forward. Suddenly my valueless stock had become very valuable.

"Then," I told Peter, "let Jeffrey know I have absolutely no intention of signing."

Did I do this because I saw a one-time opportunity to exercise some leverage, or simply out of spite? Was this the decision of a savvy business person or a golden opportunity for a wise-ass to raise the middle finger and shout the ultimate "Fuck you!" to the person who was, at that moment, my archrival?

Honestly, I just needed the money to start Magic Hat and saw this as an opportunity. I may not be the world's best business person, but when it comes to opportunity I am the smart bomb, programmed for the ammunition dump.

Jeffrey, who has always been a genius at finding cash, scrambled about and found someone willing to pay $160,000 for my shares.

Good deal or bad?

23 percent of Seventh Generation today would be worth

a small fortune. From that perspective, my rash decision seems short-sighted. However, soon after the IPO, Seventh Generation's stock tanked, and my 23 percent would have been worth next to nothing. Eventually, the price of the stock went so low that Jeffrey and investors re-acquired it and took the company private.

I try never to look back; but to me, it was a good deal for two reasons. First, it gave Magic Hat some desperately needed working capital. Perhaps more important, on a personal level it started my healing process from what had been the open wound of Seventh Generation. Until this point, I felt that someone had stolen my baby from me. And, it was still my baby! I was part-owner even if I wasn't allowed in the front door, let alone on the board of directors. Not a good position to be in. The settlement went a long way in removing my feeling that I had been raped and discarded.

Life: I Sorta Grow-Up

It is not easy to connect the first half of my life with the second. In the first half, I dubbed around, working mostly for other people and trying to figure out what I wanted to be when I grew up, then got married, fathered children, and moved to Vermont.

During the second half I either started or helped start five or six businesses, three of which are still going and account for something like $300 million in annual revenues. Many people looking at this would presume I had some sort of interest in, aptitude for, or training in business. An M.B.A. degree perhaps? My only advanced degree is from the University of Brick Walls and Hot Coals.

I didn't do well in college. Later, I became a back-to-the land hippie living in the hills of Vermont who had (then and now) no training nor aptitude for business. Among my tragic flaws, from the business perspective, is that money is not my primary motivator. (I put money at roughly #5 on my list of personal priorities, if anyone is keeping track.)

There was a turning point:

Lesson: The Woodshed

I didn't like school. And school didn't like me. At one point I attended five different schools in five years, mostly for the wrong reasons, and I finally limped out of high school and spent the next year in non-stop party mode.

I had a single motivation for going to college—to avoid being drafted during the Vietnam war. I had gotten into Parsons College in Iowa, and I drove my 3-miles-per-gallon Corvette to get there (more about my vehicles later). I lasted one year, and then went to California. After a few months in the Haight-Ashbury district of San Francisco, I came home and enrolled in Long Island University at Southampton.

Things were not pleasant at home. My parents' relationship had soured. My father—the same fun guy of my early youth—was a nonstop fountain of criticism, so I lived off-campus where my focus was, quite naturally, my buddies, girls, and partying.

An abrupt change in direction occurred early one morning when there was a banging on my door, and I awoke to the jarring sounds of two Suffolk County policemen searching my apartment. I was busted for a small amount of marijuana and some pills.

This was a much more serious matter at that time then it would be now. Depending on the outcome, I could face jail time or a felony conviction that would hinder my ability to get employment or credit. Most likely I would be expelled from school. Without school, no draft deferment. Without a draft deferment, I'd be drafted, sent to Vietnam, and end up facedown in some distant rice paddy.

In other words, I had fucked up—not that I was doing anything worse than the rest of my friends, but I had gotten caught.

It was my lawyer who took me to the woodshed and read me the riot act. Long story short: "Straighten up and fly right." Instead of blowing him off, as I might have if my father had told me the same thing, I listened. And I decided he was right.

I became involved in school activities, specifically the school newspaper and student government. I served on the judicial board—the same one that might someday be ruling on my academic eligibility. I've always loved a good irony. A funny thing happened as I became more engaged. I started liking school a little more and taking things more seriously. I focused on a major in psychology, actually started attending classes more regularly, and my grades went up. Go figure.

Meanwhile, on the legal front, the news was all good. The pills that the police had confiscated somehow disappeared. (Cops have their vices, too.) This weakened the case against me, and the charge was reduced to an "offense," which is more or less as serious as a speeding ticket.

I dodged the bullet.

My positive momentum continued in the classroom, as well, and I ultimately graduated on the Dean's List in January, 1970. All I needed now was a way to avoid the draft and being sent to Vietnam as cannon fodder.

Times: The Luck of the Draw

November 10 comes through again!

On December 1, 1969, the Selective Service System of the United States held a lottery of all draft-eligible men who were born between 1944 and 1950, to determine the order of induction into the Army. Up until this time it had been done on a year-by-year basis, meaning that you were subject to the draft every year up until the age of twenty-six.

The Vietnam war was raging, brought to us nightly by Walter Cronkite on the news. All our heroes in music and film were raging against the war. White kids were going to extraordinary lengths to avoid induction—fleeing to Canada, declaring as conscientious objectors, or abusing their bodies in horrible ways to fail their physicals. I've heard of one guy, Shepard Ogden, the founder of Cook's Garden Seed Catalog and a fellow Vermont entrepreneur, who had "FUCK YOU" tattooed on the edge of his hand so that it would show when he saluted, an extraordinarily creative yet potentially foolhardy move. How do you think boot camp would have been for him? Luckily, it got him out, and he was disqualified.

In the lottery, the days of the year including Leap Year Day were represented by the numbers from 1 to 366 written on slips of paper, each of which was placed in a separate plastic capsule. After being mixed in a shoebox, the capsules were dumped into a deep glass jar, and then drawn from the jar one at a time.

My draft-eligible friends and I gathered on the night of December 1 to watch our fates unfold. It's a time that—along with the JFK assassination and the 9/11 attack on the Twin Towers—is seared into my memory, and yet the setting was completely casual—: a bunch of couples sitting around drinking beers and passing joints. The first number drawn was 257 (September 14), so all registrants born on that day were assigned lottery number 1. Anyone between the ages of eighteen and twenty-five who was born on any of the first 195 birth dates called would have to serve.

The dynamic that night was weird, to say the least. Initially, it was tense. For those whose numbers were called, it became instantly devastating, as if someone was saying "Congratulations, you just won a death sentence."

It reminds me of the popular joke at the time: A woman opens the door to find the Western Union messenger. "I have a telegram for you," the messenger says. "Oh," says the woman. "Will you please sing it to me?"

"I'd rather not," says the messenger.

"Pull-l-l-leas-s-se," says the woman. "I've never had a singing telegram."

" Well . . . ok. Ta-da-ta-da-ta-da, your son is dead!"

Ouch. That was 1969.

As the evening wore on, the mood in the room became anticipatory, like a gambling casino, as the odds moved in our favor and we survived each passing number. After the magic number of 195 was reached, an instant party broke out. Those of us whose number hadn't been called were forever freed of the yoke (and cruel joke) of the draft.

November 10—#282—came through like a champ for me. November 9 came in at #80; November 11 at #46. If ever the meaning of "the luck of the draw" was more clear . . .

The draft lottery only intensified resentment of the Vietnam war and the draft. It strengthened the anti-war movement all over America. How could something so significant be determined by something so random? Moreover, it became increasingly understood (though largely unspoken) that as privileged whites found their ways around military service, the fighting fell disproportionately on the poor, the black, and the Hispanic. It's a disgraceful comment on this country, and, unfortunately, one that hasn't changed a lot to this day.

Nevertheless, I do breathe a sign of relief and say, "Good ol' November 10!"

In January 1970, I graduated from college and prepared for the next chapter of my life. At least I wouldn't have to worry about the interfering hand of Uncle Sam.

Chapter 5
Opportunity Knocks

*Twenty years after the first Earth Day, I find myself
with a mail-order catalog that sells the products
designed to protect the planet. As I struggle to establish
a fragile, embryonic business, little do I realize the
roller-coaster ride that is about to begin.*

Life: Looking for a Niche

I've told you how my relationship with Seventh Generation was
severed. Here's how the whole thing got started.

At Gardener's Supply we had a uniquely counter-seasonal
business for the mail-order industry where most of the
retail activity happened in the weeks immediately preceding
Christmas. Gardens, however, are planted in the spring. This
much I know about gardening. This meant that we had to
create the systems and infrastructure to handle the peak of
our business. This also meant that we had excess capacity
at the time of year when much of the mail-order business is
scrambling to fill orders.

This represented a business opportunity, of sorts.

Gardener's Supply had grown steadily during my relatively
brief period with them. Because I had put together the back-
end of the business (warehousing, shipping, computer support,
and customer service), I was a natural candidate to develop
this opportunity. Not that I necessarily shared this vision.
Today, Will Raap and I have been such longstanding business

colleagues, mutually supportive of each others' ventures, and members of the Burlington business community, that it's easy to forget that things weren't always entirely congenial between us. In fact, given the choice between staying in the bosom of the prospering Gardener's Supply and doing a start-up venture, I would have taken the bosom!

But I wasn't given that option, and now, with the benefit of hindsight, I realize that it was time for me to move on. This is often the case with terminations, no matter how painful they seem at the time. Moreover, I was treated fairly and with respect, laying the foundation for a strong continuing relationship with the company and its employees, including— and especially—Will.

(Will recently sent me some of our correspondence from this era. Even though we were dealing with some turbulent and emotional issues, what impressed me most was how unfailingly polite and considerate we were toward each other.)

Niche Marketing Services opened its doors (more accurately "door") in a small office within Gardener's Supply in 1983—84, and I began looking for more clients who needed professional fulfillment services. My first client was the mail-order catalog of a non-profit organization called Co-op America (now called Green America).

Green America, founded by Paul Freundlich in 1982, is a non-profit membership organization that promotes social justice and environmental sustainability by harnessing the economic power of consumers, investors, and businesses and connecting them in the marketplace. Their catalog was an early manifestation of this effort, which today includes publications such as the National Green Pages and events such as their Green Business Conferences.

There's always a murky territory that exists between the worlds of non-profit and for-profit organizations. It's clear enough with for-profits: their lifeblood comes from the revenues they generate from selling their products or services for an amount in excess of what it costs to deliver said products or services. Non-profits, however, have to beg. This is hard work, and it's inevitable that enterprising non-profits will seek alternative ways to generate revenues.

This has led organizations such as Green America and National Gardening into the retail or mail-order businesses, which in turn can jeopardize their non-profit status. (This, remember, is what led to the spin-off of Gardener's Supply from National Gardening.)

This inherent awkwardness was the case with the early Co-op America, but, in Mom's words, even "more so." The challenge in this case was that much of the merchandise came from their business members, meaning that the catalog was more like a farmer's market in print than a traditional mail-order business. Still . . . great organization, great people, great mission, and great challenges. I worked closely with Paul and his key staffer, Denise Hamler, to work through the logistical details. No one made a ton of money, but I made some good friends and felt like I was making the world a little better place to live.

And the relationship must have worked for them, too, because they referred another D.C.-based catalog to Niche. This was an environmental organization with a catalog of energy-saving and planet-friendly products. Their catalog, ReNew America, was filled with good information and well-intended products, but it was probably the worst catalog I've ever come across. I could immediately see a zillion ways to improve it. I shared many of these freely with the ReNew America staff. Even though they were receptive to many of the ideas, and we developed a great working relationship, they were a mission-driven activist organization, not a professional catalog company. Not only were their resources limited, but their interests lay elsewhere.

Eventually, ReNew America tried to sell me their catalog. While I was tempted by the prospect of having my own ship, it needed such a drastic overhaul that I said no. But then they came back and said "We're abandoning it. Throwing it in the garbage can. Do you want it? It's yours for the asking."

Have you ever been to the landfill, and there, next to the dumpster is an old lawn mower or something that you know is broken, but looks too good to throw away? That was the case with the ReNew America catalog. My brain told me to pass on the "opportunity," but my brain was not controlling my mouth. As if having an out-of-body experience, I heard myself uttering the fateful words: "I'll take it."

To this day I don't know why I said them. But, I'm glad I did.

Times: They Are a-Changin'

Niche was making forward progress, but I was already seeing glimmers of the fact that this was not the kind of business I would thrive in. Like my health-care consulting businesses, it was a service business, and I'm not a service kinda guy. It was a Ford Fairlane, and I wanted a Corvette—something I could get behind the wheel of and drive.

In a service business, you are basically an hourly worker renting the business. You might be paid more than a burger flipper, but your upside potential is still limited by the number of hours in the day. It's a little better than the retail business, where you are dependent on the customers coming through the door, but not by much. The customers can turn and leave through the same door for any reason.

With Renew America, I felt for the first time that I was making a personal statement of values with my business. Like all good ex-hippies, I considered myself an environmentalist. I remember the first Earth Day in 1970, which many people consider the birth of the modern environmental movement. Here's how it's described on the Earth Day Network website (earthday.org):

The height of hippie and flower-child culture in the United States, 1970 brought the death of Jimi Hendrix, the last Beatles album, and Simon & Garfunkel's "Bridge Over Troubled Water." Protest was the order of the day, but saving the planet was not the cause. War raged in Vietnam, and students nationwide increasingly opposed it.

At the time, Americans were slurping leaded gas through massive V8 sedans. Industry belched out smoke and sludge with little fear of legal consequences or bad press. Air pollution was commonly accepted as the smell of prosperity. "Environment" was a word that appeared more often in spelling bees than on the evening news. Although mainstream America remained oblivious to environmental concerns, the stage had been set for change by the publication of Rachel Carson's New York Times bestseller Silent Spring in 1962.

Earth Day 1970 capitalized on the emerging consciousness, channeling the energy of the anti-war protest movement and putting environmental concerns front and center.

Over the course of the 1970s and early '80s, however, interest in Earth Day (and the environment) had waned. Much of this was caused by the economic recession, the stock-market crash of 1987 (Black Monday), and a series of environmental disasters, including the Chernobyl nuclear disaster and the catastrophic Exxon-Valdez oil spill. The solar panels put up on the roof of a section of the White House by Jimmy Carter in 1979 were taken down by Ronald Reagan in 1986.

Environmentalists felt very much under attack. Ironically, the dismantling of the environmental gains by the Reagan administration had a galvanizing effect on the movement. The 3R's of "reduce, reuse and recycle" were gaining in acceptance and starting to alter consumer behavior. They were augmented by a host of other "re-'s" such as recharge, reinvent, rejuvenate, and renew.

By the time I became the owner of the Renew America catalog, the environmental movement was at least showing a pulse. It was no longer on life support. All we needed was a new name for the catalog.

Chapter 6
The Name Game

Nowhere is the fear factor more apparent than when it comes to naming the new business. In this chapter, "The Name Game," I reflect on my various ventures and the thought processes that went into creating them.

Lesson: A Name Is a Name, Now Move On!

Naming a company is not unlike naming a kid. Most people go through thousands of possibilities. None of them seem quite right. Then the proud parents find one they like. They sit on it for a little while, then they make the mistake of trying it out on someone.

"What do you think of 'Alan' if it's a boy?"

"Alan!" comes the response. "Sounds like a nerdy Jewish kid who has a bed-wetting problem!" So that name is crossed off the list.

"Green Mountain Coffee Roasters" is an example of a bad business name. In fact you'd have a hard time thinking up a worse one. Who thinks "coffee" in the same sentence as "the Green Mountains"? Well, maybe the Ethan Allen Olive Oil Company would be worse. Ben & Jerry's is a great name, but only in hindsight. When they started, they were widely accused of ripping off the more-established and now defunct Steve's Ice Cream of Cambridge.

Green Mountain Coffee is also an example for how

irrelevant a name becomes once a company establishes its momentum, as they have. Now, it rolls off the tongue as easily as Microsoft (the maker of blankets with high thread counts) and Apple (the fruit vendor).

Here's my secret technique for naming not only companies, but products. Hire really creative people. Have them come to a meeting with a list of suggested names. Sit Buddah-like at a conference table as they champion their ideas.

Suddenly exclaim, "That's the one." Afterward, everyone will tell you what a genius you are. Almost none of the great names that I'm associated with—Circus Boy, #9, Blind Faith, Heart of Darkness—originated in my brain.

Most people today know the origin of the name Seventh Generation—the Iroquois law that says that in all our decisions we should consider the impact on our descendants for seven generations. Today, most people think it's a great name. Not so at the time. In fact, most everyone thought it was the stupidest name they had ever heard. Here are typical responses when I tried it out on people:

"No one will know what it means."

"Too convoluted."

"Makes no sense."

"What are you? Stupid?"

So, why, given such choice feedback, did we use that name?

Time—or rather, the lack of it.

I had already "purchased" the catalog and business from Renew America. I didn't hate the name Renew America, but considered it was too "local" for my grand, international aspirations. Why would folks in the U.K. or France or Belgium want to renew America?

We needed a new name.

The first catalog was speeding toward completion, as we

were on a very tight deadline to get it out. We had the product. We had the layout. We had the copy. We had it all—everything except a name.

We had been playing the name game in the office for months. Names came from every direction. I rejected them all. We were out of time. The catalog was about ready to print and really (really!) needed a name.

So I had lunch with Lyman Wood. My agenda was, "Help! I need a name."

I have always remembered (and followed) Lyman's sage advice ever since. He said, "Alan, I've named hundreds of businesses and products over the years. Every one has sounded odd when I first used it. And every one has sounded perfect after using it for thirty days. Even more important, no name has ever caused any of my products or businesses to either succeed or fail. So pick a name and move on. It will be fine."

Armed with this advice, I went back to the office, gathered our meager staff (and whoever else was around), and started putting suggestions up on the blackboard, as I had done ten times previously. Only this time I told everyone that we were picking a name from the list before we left the room.

A woman named Denise Dunbar, who worked for Gardener's Supply Company (where we had our offices at the time) and who was part Native American, happened to be there. She suggested Seventh Generation. It went up on the board.

"Seventh Generation" won by elimination. It was the last name standing. The other names were totally unacceptable to me (and no, I don't remember any of the others today). If nothing else, Seventh Generation sounded interesting. I will choose interesting over mundane any day. And the problem of "what does it mean?" was solved by putting the whole quote from the Iroquois right next to it in smaller letters.

It has held up beautifully for a company selling

environmentally friendly products, even spanning the company's transition from a catalog company to a wholesale distributor. It has always been a great conversation starter, then and now.

It stands as exhibit A in proving the wisdom of Lyman Wood.

Life: Because Names Are Fun

"Magic Hat" has an equally interesting but entirely different story. In my seventeen years of running the company, the inevitable first question people asked me was always "Where did the company name come from?" often followed closely by "Where did the name #9 come from?"

I don't know why people are so curious about names, but they are. I've often thought we should hire a novelist or playwright to come up some really juicy stories on the origin of the names, because the actual stories are not very dramatic. However, for the record:

Magic Hat, like Seventh Generation, was chosen by a process of elimination. At the time, almost every brewery was named after either their geographic location (Long Trail, Otter Creek, Shipyard, Boston Beer Company) or their founder (Pete's Wicked Ale). Bob and I quickly nixed either of these directions. "Bob & Alan's Beer?" I don't think so.

Next to be crossed of the list was anything too Vermont-centric. I know, it's sacrilege. Everyone in the state believes in the "magic" of the Vermont brand—that is, everyone but me. As usual, I had national/international aspirations for the brand, so could not figure why someone in Birmingham, Alabama, or Blacksburg, Virginia, let alone Dublin or London, cared if the beer was from Vermont.

We knew we wanted something distinctive, something we could build a "brand" behind. We wanted a name that meant nothing, so we could make it mean whatever we pleased.

So the games began. Bob and I threw names around constantly between us, and to anyone else who would listen. Nothing stuck.

As Bob and I were driving through the Oregon hillside, visiting breweries, talking about our new business, I started talking about how business is magic, in that every business has a moment of truth when it looks like it will go down the tubes until someone pulls a rabbit out of a magic hat. Bob said, "Hmmmmm. Brewing is about alchemy – turning water, grain, and yeast into this delicious beverage. What if instead of using a 'Magic Hat' to pull out a rabbit, it becomes the source of our magic for creating beer?" We liked it, and the name settled in during the rest of that trip.

The response to the name was not unlike what I had experienced initially with Seventh Generation. Returning to Burlington from Oregon, I started talking to my friends about the trip and our brewery plans, including the name. All of them told us, "It sucks." The more I heard how everyone thought it sucked, the better I liked it.

Then, the final vote. We were working with a local (now international) design firm to develop the original logo and brand family look. At every one of the early meetings they would bitch about the name. Finally, out of frustration, I challenged them to beat it. We spent another month poring through lists of names (again!) looking for the perfect brewery name. After endless discussion, we all agreed, Magic Hat it is.

Lyman's rule had proven itself again. "Magic Hat" was an odd-sounding name, and peoples' initial reaction was negative. But as we used it over time, it became more comfortable and they came to appreciate the value in having such a distinctive name. The name worked well for us, but that was never the reason the business succeeded.

Here's the story of how our most popular beer, #9, got its name:

Originally, when this beer made its debut in 1995, it was intended as our first summer seasonal. It eventually became one of the most successful and iconic craft beer brands on the East Coast.

Before we even had a brewery, we had a company T-shirt and sponsored some local events. We even sold a little draft beer that Bob brewed at Federal Jack's Brewpub in Kennebunkport, Maine. We sponsored a local Blues Festival in Burlington to build a little pre-brewery brand buzz. That first beer we brewed was an Irish-style red ale, a tad too dark and malty for the average beer drinker at the time. "Got anything lighter?" was a common response.

For the second year of the event, we tested a new beer, much lighter and easier to drink. Because it was experimental, we wanted a suitably experimental name and called it X-1-9 (named after the Fiat sports car that I was driving at the time). It was a HUGE hit.

When it was time to introduce our first seasonal in the summer of '95, we really didn't have time to develop another beer, so Bob and I had the brilliant idea of making X-1-9 our new summer seasonal.

We tweaked and finalized the beer. We made the label. We applied for a trademark—whoops! The lawyers said we could not trademark it, because of the "X" (already in use by others, and very distinctive). Necessity once again, proved the mother of invention. We had to get the label to the printer. So #9 it was. The name struck even though it's on the stupid side, but it was distinctive enough to get people to try it, and the beer was every bit as unique as its name.

Lesson: Listen to Your Customers, Stupid!

You know, Lyman's advice that the name of a product wouldn't cause it either to succeed or fail may be wrong in this one case, because I do believe that the name of #9 may have been responsible for its success. We never had a beer like it. It came out of the gate fast and increased sales from quarter to quarter for fifteen consecutive years. That's an astounding record. Fifteen consecutive years!

However, it almost died an early death, because it was developed as a seasonal and was scheduled to be discontinued after that first summer'. When our local distributor called to order more, I told them we were done making #9 and they should order the fall seasonal. The distributor said that all hell would break loose if we stopped producing #9. I stuck to my guns. Get over it. Order the fall seasonal. Instead of arguing with me, the distributor told our top customers that we were killing #9 and, if they didn't like it, they should call me to complain. After the fifth, sixth, and seventh call from our top accounts, all threatening to cut us out of their establishments, I turned to Bob and said, "I have a brilliant idea. Let's make #9 our second year-round beer."

That, as they say, is history. (It's also the only smart thing that particular distributor ever did for us, but that's another story.)

Chapter 7
The Perfect Storm

*Now for the good stuff. We take a moment to reflect
on my love of cars and passion for driving. The primal
need to be behind the wheel, in control of your destiny,
is an essential trait for all entrepreneurs.*

*We review my entire vehicular history, from the
1958 Corvette to the Vespa motor scooter to prove the
adage "You are what you drive."*

*Meanwhile, at Seventh Generation, a perfect storm
of conditions propels young Jeffrey and Alan from
obscurity to the pages of **People** magazine and the
Wall Street Journal.*

Life: You Are What You Drive

Let's talk cars for a while.

I love to drive. Driving is a metaphor for life. Nothing quite
gives me the feeling of being in control of my own destiny than
being behind the wheel.

If I think of the perfect moments in life, the first one that
comes to mind is driving on a warm summer night in the
mid-1960s in my friend's Austin-Healey 3000 with the top
down on the Taconic Parkway heading toward his family's lake
house. The Austin-Healey 3000 is a British sports car built
between 1959 to 1967 with a low engine purr that is the most
sensual I've ever heard. It's a racing machine. We'd go out on

Friday night dates on Long Island, then head north. He liked to sleep; I like to drive. It was a completely visceral experience. Freedom.

I still love to drive. I will take a ten-hour drive over a two-hour flight any day.

When I finally got my license, I—along with every other sixteen year old male in America—wanted a Corvette. What I got instead was a hand-me-down 1957 Ford Fairlane hard-top convertible from my mother. Looking back, this was actually a cool car that I wouldn't mind owning today. It was longer, wider, lower, and sleeker than previous models, with what was called a Skyliner power-retractable hardtop, whose solid top hinged and folded down into the trunk. It took up almost all the trunk space when retracted. It was a feature that sounded better than it sold, and Ford discontinued it after a year or so.

It was probably a function of sound parental judgment to put a little metal around a new driver, but all I knew was that it wasn't my coveted "vette, so I did what every rational kid of this age would do: I tried to kill it. I'd take it on the highway, run it up to 65 miles per hour, put it into neutral, floor the accelerator, and drop the transmission into "low" gear. I refused to change the oil. I abused that car in every way possible until I successfully put it out of my misery right after graduating from high school. I had earned money from my various part-time jobs, and this time I was not to be denied. I plunked the money down on a two-tone gray 1958 Corvette that only got 3 to 4 miles to the gallon and wouldn't run on any fuel except Sunoco High Test.

(Please don't pass this on to my friends who think that I'm an enlightened friend of the environment.)

Lesson: Don't Believe What You Read, Especially About Yourself

You don't need to be a business genius to know that entering an equal partnership is not the best idea. But the institution of marriage wouldn't exist if equal partnerships were always a terrible idea.

On second thought, maybe that's why there are so many marriage jokes. Take my wife—please.

Let me explain how I came to be in an equal partnership with Jeffrey Hollender at Seventh Generation. Here's how it happened. It started when the first re-tooled Seventh Generation catalog was mailed in 1988. It was an immediate success, teaching me several important business lessons very quickly:

1. Given the choice between good timing and intelligence, choose timing.

2. Don't believe your own press releases.

3. Equal partnerships are not equal.

4. Growing businesses burn cash.

The success of the Seventh Generation catalog mailing put everything into fast-motion. I sensed that we had a real opportunity for success, and this success would never happen if I was splitting my attention between the mail-order business and Niche Marketing. I had spent three years making Niche Marketing a modestly successful operation, grossing over a million dollars in sales annually. But, it was still basically an adjunct of Gardener's Supply, whereas Seventh Generation was my own baby.

I called a meeting with some of the people who had been financially supportive of Niche to tell them I had to make a choice—Niche or Seventh Generation—but in preparing the information for others to help me decide, the decision became clear to me, and I went into the meeting with my mind already made up. Niche Marketing was a Volkswagen, while Seventh Generation was potentially a Porsche. One of my investors asked if he could bring a friend to the meeting. That's how I met Jeff Hollender.

Over the years 'the two of us have been called everything from the "odd couple" to the "dynamic duo." Superficially, we are polar opposites, but we actually share a number of commonalities. We're both from New York. He's uptown, and I'm from the "burbs of Long Island. We're both from Jewish families. He's more overtly religious than I am. That's about it for the similarities.

"Perfect storm" is a phrase that was brought into wide circulation in popular culture from the 1993 book (and 2000 movie) of the same title by Sebastian Junger, which describes a confluence of seemingly unrelated events that results in an effect or impact that is far greater than the sum of its parts. Part one of my "perfect storm" was the acquisition I made of the ReNew America catalog and its subsequent re-positioning as Seventh Generation. Part two was partnering with Jeff, who brought many needed attributes to the table, not the least of which was to provide access to the capital needed to enable explosive growth. Part three was the effect of media coverage. This is the element that none of us could have anticipated.

Within a year of creating our new partnership, Seventh Generation (and Jeff and I personally) were experiencing media coverage that couldn't have been bought by the best public-relations firm in the world. (I suspect that our PR firms from those days would take exception to this comment, but the reality was that very few of our biggest stories ever came through the PR firms.)

Remember what Bill Russell said: "You're never as good as you think you are when you're on top, and you're never as bad as you think you are when you're down and out."

We were instantly on top. The tendency when this happens is to assume that the credit is due to your personal attributes—your wisdom, good looks, perception, charm. Time—and a few good whacks to the head—bring you sufficient humility to recognize the other external figures at play. Remember "timing."

The first of these, quite simply, was the twentieth anniversary of Earth Day. The environmental movement had coalesced to use this as an occasion to revitalize the movement around the world. Under the leadership of Denis Hayes, who was the U.S. national co-ordinator of the original Earth Day, the event generated a huge amount of activity and noise that forced every paper and magazine in the country to do stories on the environment.

The second factor I call the "Ben & Jerry effect." Ben Cohen and Jerry Greenfield started making ice cream in Burlington in 1984. A few years later, they had a wildly successful public stock offering that was available only to Vermonters. They defied marketing logic in every possible way: They put their own goofy images on their packaging. They named products after rock stars. They supported social causes such as supporting subsistence farmers growing nuts in the rainforest. They took on the corporate giant Pillsbury (which owned Häagen-Dazs) in their "What's the Doughboy afraid of?" public-relations campaign.

They also, completely inadvertently, created an insatiable media demand for business stories about wacky people in Vermont enjoying unprecedented success. Jeff and I, the slick city boy with the good haircut and the barefoot guy with the beard, fit the bill perfectly.

Before long, we were in the middle of the perfect storm, having the ride of our lives and enjoying every crazy second of it. We were in People, Newsweek, and the Wall Street Journal. A story in the New York Times was syndicated to more than 100 additional newspapers around the country. The free exposure, in turn, generated new inquiries for the catalog, which generated new customers, which increased sales, which attracted more investment capital.

The environment within the business was wild, too. While Jeff remained based in New York taking care of the financial end and product development, I managed the launch of our business expansion in Vermont. We moved to a new facility in Colchester, Vermont, an industrial building which enabled us to handle the increased volume efficiently.

I was hiring new people like crazy. In an attempt to reconcile our bland Butler building setting with our company culture, I put a ping-pong table in the warehouse and made available free Ben & Jerry's. Our staff meeting room had no tables and chairs, only pillows. We had a real nap room. I tried to instill an ethic of total honesty: if you know something that is hurting this company and you say nothing, that's the same as lying. I couldn't afford to pay people double time for vacations, as Lyman Wood had, but I did institute a "Mistake of the Week" policy in which employees "competed" for who made the biggest "mistake" each week—and the mistake was rewarded with a cash prize.

And the craziest thing was . . . everything worked. The weirder and more off-the-wall my ideas were, the more business seemed to improve and the media lapped it up. There were two possible explanations:

1. It was a business environment that was so fueled by growth that even bad decisions had positive results, or

2. I was a freakin' genius who was re-inventing the business rule book.

I tried hard to maintain an orientation of modesty and humility, but I have to admit that some of this went to my head.

Jeff was, for the most part, politely tolerant of my eccentricities. He maintained his New York office. We talked several times a day on the phone, and he'd come up to Vermont every few weeks. Our partnership was productive.

Some employees grumbled about Jeff's stylistic differences and his huge (by Vermont standards) expense account, but this was a period where the positives far outweighed the negatives. In March 1989, an article in the New York Times profiled me as a guru for both the environmental world and the business world. Orders skyrocketed. By early 1990, we had increased from an average of 600 orders a week to over 7,000! The wild ride had now gone completely bonkers.

The craziness continued on the media front as well. I'm not about to go back and re-read those artifacts, but I remember Jeff being portrayed in the following terms: "intense, hard-working, dashingly handsome, intellectual, articulate," while I was "charismatic, cuddly, outspoken, and wildly innovative."

But remember what Bill Russell said.

Sales increased seven-fold in 1990. There's a business rule of thumb that every dollar of sales growth requires half a dollar of capital investment. Jeff proved more than equal to the task, raising more than $5 million. We both knew that this growth rate could not continue for long, so we were very conservative in our planning for 1991 and ratcheted our sales growth down to a mere 300 percent.

He was getting things done on the product development side, too, adding products ranging from beeswax candles to bio-degradable panty liners. We were so busy keeping up with the growth of the company that we had no time to pay attention to the rest of the world.

Things were crazy. Once we were en route to the airport for a conference in California when we found out that the conference was canceled. We decided to go anyway, thinking that a nice, long plane ride would be just what we needed to catch up on some long-range planning. We could indulge ourselves.

We were rock stars.

Life: Bush Invades Iraq! Saddam Torches Oil Wells in Kuwait!

Why didn't someone tell us that George Bush (the elder) was going to invade Iraq?

Whenever I am tempted to make excuses for the factors that reversed the fortunes of Seventh Generation, I remember the words of one of my business colleagues who said, "Strong companies can survive at least two downturns." Seventh Generation was not yet a strong company.

The perfect storm that fueled our climb fueled our descent as well. The problem was not only the war in Iraq but that the economy tanked, too. Remember "It's the economy, stupid!" George Bush went from being the president with one of the highest-approval ratings ever to one of the lowest, almost overnight.

Add to the mix that our success had attracted a host of new competitors who were after our same market segment. Also, the shot in the arm that the 20th Earth Day had given the environmental movement was now yesterday's news.

The company that was geared up for more than $20 million in sales suddenly had to plan for $15 million . . . then $10 million . . . and then—we were in free fall. No one knew where the bottom was. Loyal employees had to be let go. Investors had to be placated. The stresses on both of us were enormous, although we had different tools and strategies for handling them. Reduce, reuse, recycle . . . We needed another "re-" word. We needed to reinvent ourselves; but with all the noise in my head, I couldn't think straight.

Life: A Long Sabbatical

I had been planning on taking a sabbatical for a while, but I kept putting it off because there was always too much going on. My work at Gardener's Supply, Niche Marketing, and Seventh Generation had kept me on the entrepreneurial treadmill of eighty-hour weeks for too long. I was putting heart, soul, and energy into business at the expense of my family and myself. I was burnt-out . . . fried. I knew it; my wife, Judy knew it; everyone at Seventh Generation knew it.

There was no secret to my plan to take a sabbatical. Jeff knew about it and was generally supportive. The timing, however, was not yet determined.

The disaster that was 1991 continued during the holiday season that year. The catalog business—Gardener's Supply being a notable example—is highly dependent on the short, intense gift-giving season in December. Retailers of every kind know that the sales year might limp along all year but can be salvaged by the holidays. The selling season is even more compact in mail order, because the customer cannot walk in on December 24 for a last-minute catalog gift. In mail order, as much as 75 percent of the activity for the year takes place between the week before Thanksgiving and the two weeks following.

You'd better be ready when it comes.

Mail-order marketers have to place all their bets in advance. You have to bet how many catalogs to put into the mail stream; you have to bet what the response rate and average order will be; you have to bet what items will be hot, so as not to lose the short window of opportunity.

Our holiday catalog looked great. It was brimming with great new products and was being mailed more deeply than any we'd done before. The operations, under the direction of Steve Hood, were humming. The shelves were loaded with "merch"; the customer-service agents were in place. We were poised.

All we needed was for the postman to start delivering sacks of orders, and for the phone to ring off the hook.

America in the late fall of 1991, however, was not in much of a holiday mood. After the first Gulf War, George Bush the Elder had one of the highest popularity ratings of any president. The steep recession that followed the war, however, changed all of that. During the 1992 presidential campaign, Democratic candidate Bill Clinton used the catch-phrase, "It's the economy, stupid!" to unseat the incumbent president after just one term. The market tanked. Things were grim, and it was not a time when people were thinking in terms of saving the planet.

I was lying in bed one night, unable to sleep. The early holiday results were now clear, and they were uglier than anyone could have guessed. We faced another round of personnel layoffs, this time even including Steve Hood, who had done such a terrific job getting our operations in great shape. Moreover, because Americans don't buy a whole lot of stuff during the first eight months of the year, there was no way we would be digging ourselves out of this hole anytime soon.

I remember thinking "We're going to be hurting without Steve Hood. Meanwhile, I'm the guy who needs the rest." Suddenly it came to me: this was the time to take my sabbatical. Moreover, since my leave would be unpaid, the money saved on my salary could be used to keep Steve Hood on board.

I told Jeff I needed a break to clear my head, recharge my batteries, think through what the future would be for Seventh Generation. Six months. Jeff might remember it differently, but the way I remembered it was that, although he wasn't crazy about the company's current situation (neither was I) or about running it all by himself, he thought this was as good a time as any for me to take my break.

Neither of us wanted this downturn, and both of us knew that the causes were beyond the ability of us, as individuals, to control. Jeff, too, had resisted the temptation to jump ship, and remained committed to keeping the company going. I was equally committed, but it wasn't possible for me to stay at this moment. I had nothing left in the tank. To use Arnie Koss's airplane analogy again (see Chapter 2), I was out of gas. The immediate task was not to reach land, but to survive. My plane was in danger of going down.

There were some fundamental business differences developing between us as well. Despite our misreading of sales demand in 1991, I remained confident in the retail business. Using the skill set I had learned initially from Lyman Wood and honed by working with Will Raap at Gardener's Supply, we could adjust the product mix and creative strategy to find the right seam in the marketplace. The principles of marketing are unquestionable, and one of the beauties of catalog marketing is the flexibility to reposition the brand.

A number of new retail opportunities had been presented, too, but we had been so busy putting out fires that we hadn't had time to properly evaluate them. Despite the economic downturn, there was no shortage of people and organizations wanting to do business with us.

However, Jeff believed more in the idea of making Seventh Generation a wholesale consumer brand. He saw a potential for wholesaling private-label ecological cleaning products and recycled paper products that I didn't share. I didn't disagree with the long-term potential for this brand strategy, but I didn't agree with the timing. Back in 1992, Whole Foods did not have 300 markets spread around the country. The trends for strong, local food co-ops was in its infancy, and traditional supermarket chains were totally unreceptive to products like ours. The right distribution channels simply did not exist.

The other half of this discussion concerns margins (the percent of gross profits expressed as a percentage of selling price). The margins in mail-order average around 60 percent. For products sold at wholesale, however, the margins are tiny, in the single digits. I didn't see how a company designed to operate on mail-order margins could sell enough of its products to be successful as the product developer and wholesaler that Jeff was advocating. There just wasn't enough volume.

In hindsight, it's clear now that Jeff could point to the eventual success of Seventh Generation as a consumer brand as proof that he was right. And I could point to the length of time it took Seventh Generation to reach profitability as proof that 1992 was not the right time to embrace that strategy.

Our differences were unresolved when I went on my sabbatical, which I spent attending to parts of my life that had been totally neglected during the previous few years on the Seventh Generation roller coaster. I got re-acquainted with my daughter, Zoe, and established a foundation to our relationship that has held us in great stead ever since. I learned how to play the bass guitar, and eventually fooled around in a rock "n' roll band consisting mostly of Seventh Generation employees. I walked Church Street in my bare feet, taking in the views of the lake and the lively scene that is uniquely Burlington.

I was still entirely engaged in the fortunes of Seventh Generation, but I consciously tried to stay out of Jeff's hair. The last thing the company needed was a distraction caused by the perception of friction or disagreement at the top. I knew he was coping with a lot, but in my own way, so was I. There was never a doubt in my mind about coming back to the company. Jeff had occasionally ranted that there would be no company for me to return to, but I thought that was the anger speaking. After all, this was my baby, and I brought him in on it, no?

So, I gave him space. Myself, too.

Gradually, I felt my mojo return. I was ready to climb back into the cockpit, to walk over the coals. I developed a clearer vision of the company that Seventh Generation could become. I presented these ideas in a letter to Jeff during the spring of 1992, but he responded in no uncertain terms that I no longer had a role in the company. I was stunned. This was a complete reversal of the understanding I thought we had. He was extremely angry. Even more so.

Things became very personal. The rift was not only between us two individuals. Within the company there were many Newman loyalists; and within the entire environmental community, the rift was perceived (at least on a symbolic level) as one between money and mission.

Complicating the situation was that we were such a highly visible company as a result of our media bonanza. Not only was there the dramatic downfall of yesterday's shooting star, but, increasingly, there was the obvious conflict between the city slicker from New York and the happy hippie from Burlington. It was great local soap opera, and everyone wanted to know the behind-the-scenes story.

Things had changed, and I didn't know why. My mind reeled with speculation. I finally met with a representative of the company's board of directors (Chico Lager) to explain my position and to request the opportunity to meet with the full board to present my thinking on the company's future and my role in making it happen. I don't know whether he conveyed my request or not, but I was never given the opportunity to meet with them. My career with Seventh Generation, the company I founded, was over.

There's no point in revisiting the details of this time. Too much negativity. The wounds healed eventually, though not without scars. Although Jeff and I have each moved on and we manage to co-exist in the community of Burlington, Vermont, and the community of environmental businesses, the personal issues were never fully resolved. Initially, I felt violated, felt that something had been stolen. A lot of that feeling dissipated when my shares were bought out so that Seventh Generation could do an IPO (Initial Public Offering). Remember my story about "The Call?" (See Chapter 4.)

Time heals all wounds, and while that hasn't happened yet, hopefully there's still time.

The epilogue of this part of the Seventh Generation story is that the public stock offering happened, and things went from bad to worse. Instead of having a small group of disgruntled investors whom he knew, Jeff had a much larger group of even more disgruntled investors who couldn't care less about issues of social mission. The price of the stock plummeted. To raise cash for operations, Jeff sold the catalog assets to Gaiam (a lifestyle media and product company), retaining the Seventh Generation name. Gaiam repositioned it as the Harmony catalog, based in Colorado. To the best of my knowledge, it is still operating successfully.

The market value of Seventh Generation eventually went so low that Jeff and a group of backers re-acquired it and made it a private company. Over time, and fueled by consumers' more widespread demand for earth-friendly products, Seventh Generation has realized the vision of becoming a successful brand. The company was recently cited for being the top "green" brand in America.

Along the way, Jeff Hollender has positioned himself as a prominent advocate for corporate social responsibility, the person who can bridge the gap between established corporate interests and the notion that a business can be about more than a single bottom line. He has that crossover credibility that can be accepted at Wal-Mart in a way that Alan Newman—with his beard, bare feet, and yellow glasses—never could. Jeff has written books, given keynote speeches, built a great company, and raised a wonderful family. He's grown tremendously as a business leader and, I'm sure, as a person. He has much to be proud of.

Late in 2010, the Seventh Generation's board of directors (a group that includes Jeff's wife, Sheila) informed him that his services were no longer needed. Against his will, he was forced from the company that he had nurtured and grown. I don't pretend to know the story-behind-the-story. But I did receive an endless stream of e-mails, many starting with the word "Karma."

I can't help but wonder, however, if his own experience of being forced out of a company that he nurtured and loved has given him a greater sense of empathy for what I went through in the summer of 1992.

Chapter 8
Bucky and Lyman

I wasn't much of a student, but once I put school behind me, I had some great teachers. R. Buckminster Fuller taught an entire generation how to think outside the box, while at Gardens for All, Lyman Wood taught me how to think inside the box. Their combined influences established the foundation for the business philosophy that guides me to this day.

I'm not an intellectual. I like to do things rather than theorize and debate them. I like to drive.

I do know, however, that something weird happened in the mid-1960s. Sunspots? Alien spacecraft? I don't know, but suddenly, as the Jefferson Airplane told us, "One pill makes you larger and one pill makes you small. And the one that Mother gives you won't do anything at all."

The whole world went crazy, and things were not as they seemed. I don't fully get it, but my book collaborator, Stephen Morris, attributes some of the change to the Gaia Theory. I'll let him explain it:

The Gaia Hypothesis
explained by Stephen Morris

The penny dropped for atmospheric scientist James Lovelock in the mid-1960s when he viewed the first pictures of the planet Earth taken from outer space. The Earth is not an orb of inert minerals inhabited by a few living organisms. The Earth is a living organism with all its components connected through a bewildering but awe-inspiring series of interwebbed connections.

The Gaia Theory, articulated in a series of books and articles by Lovelock over the next four decades, often in collaboration with widely respected biologist Lynn Margulis, is either the breakthrough perception of our time or, as critic Massimo Pigliucci describes it in The Skeptical Inquirer, "a hopeless mix of pseudoscience, bad science, and mysticism."

The hypothesis, named for the Greek goddess of Earth, was new enough and dramatic enough that even Lovelock admits that for the first ten years after the penny dropped he could not explain it. Over time and through repeated iterations of articulation, however, it has evolved into a theory, still controversial, but credible enough to frame important debates such as the one currently raging over global warming.

The relevance of Gaia is this: If the Earth is a living organism, then it will behave as one and will seek to maintain stasis or balance. As expressed by Lovelock "The Earth is a self-regulating system made up from the totality of organisms, the surface rocks, the ocean and the atmosphere tightly coupled as an evolving system." Accordingly, the planet will "regulate surface conditions so as always to be as favorable as possible for contemporary life."

Space exploration has been minimal in the forty-odd years since Lovelock's initial observation, but Gaia Theory has migrated from the lunatic fringe to the borderline mainstream. Half a century—that's about right as a time frame for a revolutionary new idea to gain acceptance. As we learn more about "what man hath wrought" in his creation of the circumstances that have led to the creation of the condition known as global warming, the only certainty is that the answer for "un-wroughting," if it is even possible (Lovelock himself thinks we are beyond the limits), will come from a deeper understanding of Gaia.

Times: Bucky

I took my intellectual cues from "Bucky" Fuller. In his 1970 book *I Seem To Be a Verb*, R. Buckminster Fuller wrote: "I live on Earth at present, and I don't know what I am. I know that I am not a category. I am not a thing – a noun. I seem to be a verb, an evolutionary process – an integral function of the universe."

Like Madonna, Elvis, or Prince, Fuller was big enough to be known universally to my generation by his nickname, "Bucky." Part of his theory is that all things are organic, and all things have a pattern. They get bigger . . . and bigger . . . and bigger . . . then suddenly get smaller. And this theory applies to ANYTHING, for example:

> ► in electronics – all electronics started with "tubes," and the TVs, radios, computers, and phones of the time just kept getting bigger . . . and bigger . . . and bigger, and then a new invention (transistors?) comes along and electronics get smaller again – but then start getting bigger again . . . and bigger . . . and bigger . . . then always get smaller again, thus starting the process over again.

► in business; I find this principle translated into "trends." For instance, in retail, when I was growing up, stores were small, local, and independent businesses that offered specialty items. Large department stores were few and located mostly in downtown areas. But, as time went on, retail stores got bigger and bigger, finally giving rise to the "big box" stores which are now going through another transformation, back to the smaller specialty stores. Even Walmart, king of the superstores, with all things for all people, is now building smaller stores with fewer categories. Specialty bookstores are staring to reappear in the wake of the closing of hundreds of Borders stores. The same trend is happening with specialty clothing stores, too.

► in economics – again, all things change. There was a time twenty years ago when we thought the Japanese would eventually own all American real estate. They had deals everywhere in the world. They even financed the restoration of the Sistine Chapel in return for exclusive photographic and filming rights. Their holdings were getting larger and larger in the mid-1980s, until they went bust in 1991 and sold almost everything. Then the Arabs stepped in and started buying up United States real estate, buying more, and more – then stopped, and started selling. Now it's the Chinese buying more and more. Some people are concerned that the Chinese will end up owning the whole country. Not I. This too shall pass, as it always does.

Life: The Lyman Wood Era

My real-life Bucky Fuller, a person who helped me understand things, was Lyman Wood.

Lyman Wood died on December 31, 1996 at the age of 86. I was out of town and could not get back for the funeral, so I missed my opportunity to give him a proper good-bye. I still regret that I missed that opportunity.

He was actively at work on several business projects up until his death. My kinda guy. His obituary in the New York Times, published the day after, noted that "Mr. Wood's life was marked by an untiring passion for ideas, ranging from small, quirky items to grand-scale solutions for humanity." Amen.

There are few people I look up to with unreserved admiration. Lyman was one.

Lyman founded his first company (selling candy and washing cars) at the age of thirteen. Over the next seven decades he marketed everything from portable postage scales to prayers. Early in his career, he ran a mail-order business offering prayers for a nickel. I love the visual of a large room, filled with women at tables, all furiously writing out prayers by hand. Talk about good old American manufacturing!

His first big success came in 1944 with a book called "The Have More Plan," which offered tips on living simply and thriftily to a wartime nation weary of deprivation. It was successful when it was published, and in later years it had a huge renaissance and became one of my bibles during my hippie (back to the land) years.

His partner in this venture was Ed Robinson, a New York ad executive who, along with his wife, Carolyn, recognized the strong appeal of living simply, peacefully, and abundantly off the land. The book was advertised in small ads in a wide variety of specialty publications, using a variety of headlines and customer propositions. Lyman's #1 rule for direct-response marketing was test, test, test.

His formula for success was simple but ingenious: Test the ad; measure the results; adjust accordingly; repeat the process ad infinitum. Over the years, more than half a million copies of the book have been sold, and it is still in print through Storey Publishing, another one of Lyman's many (interconnected) business offspring.

The "Have More" Plan was a useful reference for the home gardener, but usefulness alone did not explain its success. What

Wood and Robinson were selling was not a book so much as the dream of an independent life in the country. (Note to self: sell the sizzle, not the fat.) A second edition came out in 1948–49 that added references for further reading. Many of the references and chapters were republished as pamphlets that eventually became the very popular Country Wisdom series.

Wood's publishing efforts eventually led to the founding of the Garden Way Company in the 1960s. The company's mainstay product was the Troy-Bilt Roto-tiller, which the company distributed by selling directly to consumers.

The Troy-Bilt is a good product but not a likely one to be selling via mail order. It was big and heavy, and therefore hard to ship—and it was also expensive, making it hard to close a sale with a simple "advertisement." This, however, is where Lyman excelled. Using his technique of test/measure/adjust, he catapulted Troy-Bilt into a national brand with an almost cultlike following of loyal customers. The magic that Lyman had discovered is that direct marketing enables you to establish a more intimate relationship and foundation of trust with a customer. Back in those days there was less talk of "branding" than there is now, but it's the same thing.

In the world of Lyman Wood, once you had the loyal, trusting customer, the logical thing to do was to find more things to sell. This is where the Lyman Wood School of Entrepreneurism kicked into overdrive, and he started new companies to sell his customers garden products, gardening information, and a million things in between—including setting up a non-profit organization solely to increase the number of gardeners so he could sell more tillers.

But there was something more, something intangible, something that sets Lyman apart from other great entrepreneurs. He began talking about the "garden way of living." Part of it was walking the walk. Lyman developed many of his products at the experimental vegetable gardens near his home in Charlotte, Vermont. But equally important to Lyman was the way you conduct your business, an ethic of doing business that included employees, customers, and the environment. His terms for the resulting business practices were "not for profit only" and "doing well by doing good." You don't have to listen too hard to hear the mantra of the "triple bottom line." He was the first successful businessman I ever heard even use these terms, applied to a business.

One small example, but one of my favorites, was his policy of paying employees double salary when they were on vacation. His rationale was irrefutable. Your bills don't take a vacation. Your mortgage doesn't take a vacation. If you still have to meet all your regular financial obligations, then how are you going to have the money to do the fun stuff that vacation is supposed to be all about. Simple: when you went on vacation, you got two checks—one to cover your regular expenses, the other to enjoy your vacation. How cool is that!

It's not surprising that policies such as that engendered fanatical employee loyalty throughout Garden Way, where he was always known, reverently, by his first name only—just like Bucky was.

I was a latecomer to the world of Garden Way. I was hired as "THE computer guy" in 1981 at Gardens For All, the non-profit that Lyman created in 1972 to promote vegetable gardening and community gardens in Vermont and then throughout the United States. Like so many of his ventures the line between non-profit and "not-for-profit only" was fuzzy.

By the time I joined the organization, it was co-managed by Jack Robinson (son of the "Have More" author, Ed) and Will Raap, a blond, energetic young Californian with an advanced degree in city planning. I may not have their titles correct, but functionally Jack was president and Will was vice president and marketing director. Both men were steeped both in gardening and the business aura of Mr. Wood. I worked primarily for Will on the nuts and bolts of the catalog business. I didn't share either Jack's or Will's belief that the salvation of the world lies in getting more people to garden, but I did begin to become engaged in the business theories and practices of this Lyman character.One day an unassuming old guy (probably about the age I am now) came in the office. "Who's the old guy?" I asked. "Lyman Wood." I introduced myself, and from then on, whenever he showed up at the office, I'd find an excuse to spend some time with him. I wanted to hear firsthand his theories of business, and with Lyman you didn't have to ask twice.

The more I learned, the more engaged I became. Business began to make sense to me, not only financially, but as a way to engage socially and even politically. There was a cause and effect between what you did with your marketing dollar and what it returned to you. I also picked up all the direct-mail jargon: lifetime customer value, acquisition rate, return per square inch, etc.

You can learn the basics of direct marketing in a very short time. Executing them consistently over time is where the difficulty comes. Add to these basic building blocks of business the elements of evaluating, motivating, and managing people, then tying it altogether on a stage that is bigger than business— that's where it becomes really fun. And I owe a huge debt to Lyman Wood for making it all fall into place for the very first time. It wasn't long before I, too, was saying "Lyman says . . . "

My opinion of the beloved founder was not universally shared at Troy-Bilt, located in Troy, New York, where Lyman's social innovations were regarded as being at odds with the more nuts-and-bolts needs of a manufacturing company. Remember: the money folks always win. He was eventually ousted in an unfriendly takeover in 1982, but that's a mere footnote to the entire Lyman Wood story.

I always love the part in movies such as American Grafitti and, more recently, The King's Speech when the closing credits tell you what became of the main characters. Here's a brief epilogue for Garden Way: In 1993, Vermont's Governor Howard Dean honored Lyman Wood for serving as a mentor to the state's entrepreneurs and helping foster $500 million a year in state industry.

Another outgrowth of Garden Way, the National Gardening Association, was forced to spin off its catalogue division, largely due to the aggression of Smith & Hawken. This became Gardener's Supply Company, founded by Will Raap. Jack Robinson took his Garden Way background to Winslow Management Company, an investment company he founded in 1983 with the mission of demonstrating that an environmentally focused strategy could yield positive results for clients.

Other Garden Way "alumni/ae" started Storey Publishing Company (John Storey), Country Home Products (Bill Lockwood), and Vermont Teddy Bear (John Sortino). Check out the management of nearly every other prominent business in the state and it's likely that you will find a Garden Way/ Lyman Wood connection before looking very far.

If the state of Vermont ever decides to turn Camel's Hump into a Green Mountain version of Mount Rushmore, I will nominate Lyman Wood to be the first face carved there. Although his name is far from a household word, his influence on the economy and culture of not only the state but the nation is undeniable.

If you'd like more information about Lyman, the best source for that is probably a book about him and Garden Way by Roger Griffith, What a Way to Live and Make a Living: The Lyman P. Wood Story (In Brief Press, 1994). Either that or sit over a few beers with any of the charter members of the Garden Way Alumni Association.

Chapter 9
Firewalker

I reflect back on the crazy summer I spent working at the Hilltop Inn with the likes of Norman Mailer and the Velvet Underground. I connect this, however tenuously, with a course called "Money & You" that teaches me that there does not have to be a disconnect between financial success and personal values. The biggest obstacle to success for most entrepreneurs is fear. A gangly guy named Tony Robbins helps me come to grips with my own fears in a dramatic demonstration that culminates in me walking, barefoot, across a bed of glowing coals.

The entrepreneur must learn to experiment fearlessly. Bean counters and market analysts mostly look to the past and straight line the future. To them every new idea means "risk"—and risk is to be avoided at all costs. The entrepreneur knows that nine of the ten ideas may not work—but, ahhh, that one idea that does!

Times: The Hilltop Inn

This story has no relevance that I can think of to my business career. I include it only so that I can name-drop a few famous people. Plus, it adds to the texture of the story.

It was the summer of 1967. I needed money to cover my

legal bill after getting busted by the Suffolk County police. A friend of mine said he could get me a job where he worked, at the Hilltop Inn in Sag Harbor out on eastern Long Island, in the Hamptons. It was a ramshackle place, on the top of a hill (duh!) owned by a gay dentist from New York City, known by everyone around there as "Doc." This was still a time when gay people stayed pretty much under the radar.

Doc was also the dentist of the manager of the Velvet Underground—the house band at Andy Warhol's Factory, who were featured at his Exploding Plastic Inevitable events. Although the band was never a huge commercial success, many (me included) regard them as one of the most important musical influences of the 1960s. Among their members were Lou Reed (who grew up around the corner from me), John Cale, and the original 1960s femme fatale, Nico.

Doc exchanged dental care for the whole band in return for them playing rock 'n' roll for a month in the summer, and so the band came out to Hilltop to play on weekends. They were our house band, as well as Andy Warhol's. Actually, that summer, they stayed for the entire month of July. (The Inn was only open to the public on weekends.)

The weekdays were pretty relaxed at the Hilltop. I remember sleeping a lot, hanging out in bars, going to the beach—the kinds of things you should be doing when you're not quite twenty-one. The work week started at 9 a.m. on Friday, and continued nonstop until the last guest left around 9 p.m. on Sunday. And I do mean "nonstop." Doc would appear periodically at the most opportune moments, usually late night/early morning (4 a.m.). We'd open our mouths and he'd pop in a little white pill to keep us going.

I was a bit player in an amazing scene. The Inn was a safe haven for the gay community from the city, so they would show up in force, and the Velvet Underground attracted the full spectrum of crazy people from the art world. It quickly got so weird that weird became normal. There was a contingent of gay hairdressers from New Jersey, some of whom were transvestites and could transform themselves into drop-dead gorgeous babes. One of the favorite pastimes of the staff was to watch one of the Inn's straight guests put the make on one of the "babes" until the inevitable moment of truth occurred.

It was beyond crazy. It was a swirling cauldron of bizarre behavior.

Then, as if things weren't crazy enough, novelist Norman Mailer, showed up. He was making a movie nearby. (I felt like I was watching a movie the whole time I was there.) In the Hamptons, Hilltop had already established itself as a hang-out for crazies. Now, a bunch of Hollywood types were added to the scene. One night in the bar, Norman had a little too much to drink (hard as that may be to believe) and became belligerent. He ended up in a fistfight with actor Rip Torn on the barroom floor.

I had a front-row seat. It was fascinating both creatively and visually. I was engaged in what was going on, but never felt threatened. I observed, but stayed detached.

Actually, after some reflection, I've realized how this episode was relevant to my business career. First, the visual richness of Hilltop and its events has always stayed with me. I'd like to think it's something I've always brought to the table in all my ventures. Second, there's the idea that outrageous can be normal. When Seventh Generation was taking off, we instituted a number of "outrageous" (by normal standards) business practices. We had an employee nap room and a ping-pong room. We had a weekly prize for the employee who made the biggest mistakes.

The more outrageous we became, the bigger our success, at least for a while. I thought I was a visionary, a creative genius. It turns out it was just a growth environment where everything clicked, outrageous or not. When the market leveled off, suddenly I wasn't such a creative genius.

Oh, well, easy come, easy go.

Soon after my Hilltop adventure, I met my soon-to-be (and now ex-) wife, Judy. She didn't believe my lurid tales of what went on at Hilltop. Luckily, that November, we were invited to a Thanksgiving party that was a reunion of the inn's guests and staff. It was just as crazy at that party as it had been over the summer. Judy stared at the bacchanal unfolding in front of us in disbelief. I remember her muttering "Now, I believe every word you said!"

Back at Gardener's Supply Will and I had absolutely no experience for what we were about to undertake. So learning was in high gear. There were really two critical things I took away from those early Gardener's Supply Company years: the meaning of business, beyond the bottom line; and how to communicate a message to a potential customer.

In the early years, Gardener's Supply did not do the level of business we had anticipated, and everything cost more than we had anticipated. Duh! I learned this lesson over and over. But in those early days, Will and I were generally the last two people left in the office. When everyone was gone, I remember many late-night conversations where he and I would talk about the "meaning of business." When there is no money to be had, rational people need a reason to continue.

Will, being the far more philosophical of the two of us, would talk about how we were spending far more time at work, with each other, than at home with our families—and that there had to be a reason to make this worthwhile,—a bigger goal than just making money. I was game. And he starting talking bout bringing our personal values into the business workplace:— treating employees like we would treat our neighbors, and creating a bigger mission for the business than a return on investment for the shareholders (and, since we were the shareholders, we could do these things——subject to the bank covenants that came later). I can't say I always followed what he was saying in that conversation, but I liked what I was hearing;

it was a way I could relate to a business. Then came "Money and You"—a true game changer for me.

Lesson: Money and You

"Socially responsible business" as a concept has taken hold in Vermont unlike anywhere else in the country. The state's trade association (Vermont Businesses for Social Responsibility, or VBSR) has more than seven hundred members and is the second-largest trade organization in the state—only the Vermont Chamber of Commerce is larger.

A lot of people get mentioned when the conversation turns to who originated the idea of socially responsible business—Lyman Wood, Ben Cohen, Matt Rubin, me—but the guy who, in my opinion, lit a fire under the movement was Marshall Thurber. He certainly put me on a path that altered my business career.

Thurber is, according to his website, "a successful attorney, real estate developer, editor, businessman, educator, scholar, inventor, negotiator, author, visionary and public speaker." No less a luminary than R. Buckminster Fuller is quoted as having said, "Marshall Thurber is an evolutionary event in our time."

To which I will add my own endorsement (and he's welcome to use this on his website): "Marshall Thurber is a piece of work." He is currently pushing something called the Positive Deviant Network.

Shortly after starting Gardener's Supply Company, Will Raap attended Thurber's seminar called "Money and You" and came back telling me that it was something I really should check out. Thurber was running the Burklyn Business School, which he co-founded in the late 1970s to teach (again, from his website) "the global principles of cooperation learned from Dr. R. Buckminster Fuller and the contextual principles of the human potential movement," featuring techniques for maximum memory retention, simulations, music, and catchy graphics. Thurber as a teacher was effective, fun, memorable, and provocative.

At the time , an assemblage of local entrepreneurs called The Mountain Group was meeting informally. Many of the participants became my peers, mentors, and colleagues, and the attendance roster is like a "who's who" of Vermont business— Will, Ben, Jerry, Peter Asch of TwinCraft, Bill Schubart of Resolution, Hinda Miller and Lisa Lindall of Jogbra—the list goes on and on.

The news of Thurber's "Money and You" seminar swept through this group like wildfire. Maybe I was more impressionable, gullible, or susceptible, but I became one of Marshall Thurber's most enthusiastic promoters.

Like any good business person, Marshall kept coming up with new products to appeal to the people who were satisfied with their "Money and You" experience. There was his advanced seminar, called "Secrets," that I took a pass on, but I did attend one of the annual conferences that was held at Windstar, a retreat center in Colorado owned by folksinger John Denver.

Sharing the bill with Thurber was Tom Crum, an Aikido master, who was also John Denver's personal bodyguard. This was surprising in itself, as Crum is not a large man, but I guess when your are an Aikido master, you don't have to be. Crum's role was to lead us through physical exercises that paralleled the more spiritual message of Thurber's presentation.

The third presenter was a young, tall, gangly, and thoroughly likable guy named Tony Robbins, who later became famous as a self-help author and success coach. His presentation that day was "Fear into Power," about how we could harness the power of our fears and turn them into drivers of our business (or personal) success.

This resonated strongly with me, because whatever bluster

and bravado an entrepreneur presents, fear is always floating just below the surface. How am I going to make payroll? What if the new product flops? What if the bank calls the loan? How will I succeed when I have no clue what I am doing? And what will happen when everyone around me figures out I don't have a clue what I am doing?

A short digression: There are two types of people in the world when it comes to fear. At one end of the extreme is the person who is paralyzed by fear and who is unable to take a step forward unless they know the outcome in advance. This type of person never moves. At the other end is the person who plunges forward without giving a thought as to the consequences. This type of person is an excellent candidate for the crash and burn.

The entrepreneur is closer to the plunger than the cripple, but the good entrepreneur at least considers the consequences before starting the airplane's engine (to hark back to Arnie Koss's story in Chapter 2).

Robbins was right on the money in recognizing the role that fear plays in our decision-making process. Often, the situation that makes us fearful is the result of an overwhelming number of smaller problems. Individually, the problems can be solved. Collectively, however, they overwhelm.

The solution, according to Robbins, is simply to recognize the fear, break down the situation into its component parts, solve the smaller problems one at a time, and "fake it till you make it." This method of dealing with fear has proved incredibly helpful to me throughout my business career. I've even embellished Robbins's basic advice with a few nuances of my own: When you are afraid, don't stand still—keep moving. Just put one foot in front of the other and take the first step. Don't worry about what's going to happen on the fifth step, just take them one at a time.

The culmination of this workshop was a firewalk, in which

we were all required to walk barefoot over a bed of hot coals. Firewalking has become a not uncommon exercise in team building now, but in the mid-1980s it was unheard of.

"How did we do that?" Speculation ranged from mass hypnosis to outright trickery. Was Robbins some kind of sorcerer? Was it an illusion?

No one had an explanation. All we knew was that the fire was hot and those coals were real. Robbins gave us the confidence to step forward and to keep walking. Nothing before or since has given me the same skill level, confidence, and power to deal with my own fear.

Will Raap on "Money & You" and Alan

I never considered myself an entrepreneur. I had worked for a California lobbying group and an urban-planning consulting organization before living and working in the U.K. for eighteen months, including time with an international development N.G.O. After returning to the U.S. in 1977, I wanted to find work that would be "good for the planet." This was during the era of the first energy crisis, the emergence of the environmental movement and when Small Is Beautiful, Economics As If People Mattered was an international best seller.

I found work in Vermont with Garden Way, a 1,400-employee, socially responsible business whose founder Lyman Wood advocated a "not for profit only" business philosophy. After four years at Garden Way, I arrived in Troy, New York one cold January day for my first board and shareholder meeting, and a big surprise. Lyman and almost all the Vermont managers had been terminated in a cold-hearted internal coup: 53 percent of the non-Vermont shareholders did not accept Lyman's commitment to employee ownership and a larger social mission, so they fired us. I needed to either find a new job (this during the recession of the early 1980's) or start a new business. I chose to explore the new business route.

I could do the standard business planning exercise, but I really wanted the new business to take up where Garden Way had left off: a mission-driven, socially responsible business that could succeed in the market and achieve broad employee ownership. Garden Way had failed to achieve broad and deep internal alignment with its stated mission, thus precipitating the internal coup. I wanted to find out how to do this.

This pursuit led me to a three-day workshop called "Money and You" in the summer of 1983. I had a deep experience at this workshop, personally and professionally, about what was important in life and in business and the values that can help us fulfill these deeper urges while still performing in the marketplace. "Money and You" was not about money per se. It emphasized the principles of abundance and alignment: do what you are inspired to do and the money will follow, set a course that is clear and motivated people will join you, operate to add value in the world while serving market needs. Plus—and this was my biggest lesson, and it changed how I led Gardener's Supply in the early years—find ways to set and maintain an organizational "context" (values, relationships, continual aligning) to keep the larger business mission alive and progressing.

I came back from the "Money and You" seminar and wanted to share these realizations with all twelve employees who we had attracted to work at Gardener's Supply. So over the course of the next year, most of these employees were supported to take the workshop. Several also had deep experiences there, and we had a new common language to guide us in the frenzy of a new business finding its way. We worked on the human dynamics needed to help strengthen our business mission and values, deal with feelings that might limit one's power, and find interpersonal alignment while also getting stuff done. We explored how to deliver more than customers expected, how to learn from mistakes and get better, and how to build a leadership team with a full complement of skills and personality types to achieve more balanced management.

As a key manager and founder, Alan took the "Money and You" seminar with the first wave of employees. I remember he also had a deep experience. He came back softer personally and more interested in the process of building a healthy, value-adding business. He even quit smoking and adopted a healthier lifestyle! He also decided he wanted to be more involved in setting the course of Gardener's Supply versus only focusing on his role as head of operations.

Had "Money and You" unleashed Alan's entrepreneurial passions and interest as it had for me? I think it helped, and a growing new business could not accommodate two envisioning, driving personalities. It took us a year to find Alan's operations-management replacement and another year to agree and structure an "intrapreneurial" transition path for Alan. But we succeeded, aided I think by the commitment unlocked at "Money and You" to operate from integrity in our relationship. Alan then launched Niche Marketing Services, initially using Gardener's Supply's phone, computer, and warehousing infrastructure. Niche Marketing Services then morphed into Seventh Generation, and Alan was off running his own fast-growing show.

Chapter 10
The Karamel of the Korn

I become a hippie and soon thereafter make my first abortive effort at being a business owner. I learn the Karamel of the Korn, and learn that I am not a born retailer. Somehow this recollection is made relevant to my realization in 1993 that my future would be in beer. (It made sense at the time.)

Bob Johnson and I decide to open a brewery, but the breakthrough moment comes when we realize that it doesn't have to be just about beer. It is about brand and lifestyle. Magic Hat is born.

Times: Haight-Ashbury, fall 1966

Like so many interesting things in my life, it happened by chance, and I didn't see the significance until much later.

By dint of fate ("dint" meaning "force" or "power"— something I remember from my old Latin classes), I spent about two months in San Francisco's Haight-Ashbury district in the fall of 1966, long before the area hit the front cover of Time magazine.

Haight-Ashbury is a neighborhood of nineteenth-century multi-story wooden houses which became a haven for hippies in the late 1960's. Real-estate values had plummeted there due to a proposed freeway, and this translated into cheap rooms and apartments.

College kids, pot smokers, runaways, and lunatic fringers attracted by omnipresent cannabis, legal LSD (acid by Owsley), and a new kind of rock 'n' roll began streaming into the Haight for spring break of 1967. The more San Francisco's government leaders did to stop the influx, the more attention they drew from the media, a classic case of governmental miscalculation. By the time Hunter S. Thompson labeled the district "Hashbury" in the New York Times Magazine, the rush was on.

Music was everywhere. The neighborhood was home to such rock groups as the Grateful Dead, Big Brother and the Holding Company (backing Janis Joplin, a hot Texan with a HUGE voice), and the Jefferson Airplane (by that time featuring Grace Slick, another singer with a big voice), who immortalized the scene in the song "White Rabbit": "One pill makes you larger, and one pill makes you small . . . " Add the Diggers to the scene—a local "community anarchist" group known for its street theater and free food—and the stage was set for the kids to run wild.

While the energy was real, it was the media and the social scientists who propelled the subculture of the Haight into the national spotlight. When this occurred, culminating in the "Summer of Love" in 1969, it turned out that, like all good movements, the Haight was well past its peak (and I was long gone). This seems to be the way things go. Any movement with a spark of freshness and originality that hits the mainstream media ends up being so overexposed that it becomes an overnight cliché.

But in the fall of '66, the Haight was heaven on earth. No adults dared enter. "Wake and bake" was the motto of the day. Impromptu music (festivals, by today's standard) broke out on a regular basis in Golden Gate Park (at the western end of the Haight) and at the natural amphitheater atop Mount Tamalpais in Marin County, just across the Golden Gate Bridge. This was in addition to the regular evening concerts at the Fillmore West and the Cow Palace.

Days started around noon and were taken up with "hanging out," searching for food, listening to music, and talking about how to end the war in Southeast Asia. Mostly, it was an endless party. All "residents" were on the same wavelength. And that cultural moment WAS a wave.

Like all good things, however, before long the scene in the Haight had lost its edge as a counterculture utopia. Tourists, even military personnel from nearby bases, started crowding in. Overdoses, overcrowding, hunger, crime, and (later on) AIDS became the daily themes. Long-term residents started sending out the message, "Don't come here. The Revolution is over. Go home."

The Haight fell into a long period of sad decline, although the corner of Haight and Ashbury streets is still a destination for tourists, like Abbey Road in London, where they flock to have their pictures taken. The neighborhood has experienced a bit of a renaissance now, perhaps sparked by the opening of a Ben & Jerry's Scoop Shop there in the early '90s.

However, the memory that I will cherish forever is not directly from the Haight, but from Mount Tamalpais, the highest peak in Marin County, between the towns of Mill Valley and Stinson Beach. Most of the mountain is within protected public lands, including Mount Tamalpais State Park and Muir Woods. On Sundays, this was the site for free rock concerts, featuring "unknown" bands that instantly became national acts, including Country Joe and the Fish, Quicksilver Messenger Service, and Moby Grape. The freedom of that scene . . . the beauty of the headlands, the fresh air from the Pacific, the headiness of the drugs, and the feeling that anything was possible—those are my takeaways.

Making the world into our utopian ideal seemed easily within reach in 1966.

Life: The Karma of KaramelKorn

Like all good hippies, we read the popular tomes of the day, from Kurt Vonnegut's novels to the Kama Sutra. One of the concepts that we were introduced to was "karma." This is basically "what goes 'round, comes 'round." But here (from buddhanet.net) is a more rounded definition:

"In this world nothing happens to a person that he does not for some reason or other deserve. Usually, men of ordinary intellect cannot comprehend the actual reason or reasons. The definite invisible cause or causes of the visible effect is not necessarily confined to the present life, they may be traced to a proximate or remote past birth.

"According to Buddhism, this inequality is due not only to heredity, environment, 'nature and nurture,' but also to Karma. In other words, it is the result of our own past actions and our own present doings. We ourselves are responsible for our own happiness and misery. We create our own Heaven. We create our own Hell. We are the architects of our own fate."

Like I say, "What goes 'round . . . "—and most of the time, shockingly quickly.

The apple doesn't fall from the tree. Maybe so, but in my case, the first apple falls as far away from the tree as it possibly can. A strange thing happened in my family as I passed through my teens into my early twenties. My father, the family's primary caregiver and my best pal when I was a kid, became increasingly critical. I wonder why? Long-haired, pot-smoking, anti-war, counterculture—wasn't that everything a father wants in a son? I spent less time at home. He actually moved out and separated from my mother. Eventually came the divorce, to the surprise of absolutely no one.

At that point, my mother, the source of so much of my early anger, started becoming my good friend. Neither of us were very good sleepers, so on the relatively rare occasions that I was home it was not unusual for me to wander in around 3 a.m. and head down to the kitchen where I'd find her happily repotting her beloved houseplants.

We talked. We got to know each other, and we started to like each other. She became my biggest fan and supporter.

Judy and I married in September of 1969. That's what you did in those days. You found someone compatible, and if you were of the "marrying age" you got married. It was a good decision at the time. In today's world, it probably wouldn't have happened. Times change.

In December came the draft lottery, and my ticket out of military service; then, graduation in January 1970. We needed a plan and we had one. To quote Eric Burdon and the Animals, "We gotta get outta this place."

Judy and I took off, tiny trailer in tow, to find a place to live. We plotted a northern route to explore Canada. Even though there was no longer a draft to avoid, America was leaving a sour taste in the mouths of most of the people my age that I knew. The trip was great, but inconclusive in terms of where to live. After two months, we found ourselves in a commune in Eugene, Oregon. We seriously considered staying, but something vaguely wasn't right, so we abruptly packed our tent and took off for Vermont, where a friend's sister offered us a place to stay.

The house where we visited, and stayed initially, was the guest cottage of Scott and Helen Nearing. When I tell this to people today, I can tell their age and previous inclinations based on whether they are clueless or impressed—i.e., as if we were invited to stay at the Lincoln Bedroom. Scott and his wife Helen co-authored the book Living the Good Life: How to Live Simply and Sanely in a Troubled World (originally published in 1954, and more recently by Schocken Books in 1990). The book denounces the war, famine, and poverty of the modern world, extols the virtues of their homesteading experiment in Vermont, and teaches how to build stone structures with a method they invented (and which almost anyone could use, regardless of their masonry skills). Along with "The Have More Plan" and the Whole Earth Catalog, this was one of the formative tomes of the hippie tribe.

The shock waves of the 1960s had initiated a new "back-to-the-land" movement in the 1970s, which brought hundreds of would-be homesteaders to Vermont to learn country survival skills from the Nearings. Luckily for us, they had recently picked up and relocated their homestead to the coast of Maine, leaving their house available for the likes of us.

Judy and I would likely have been comfortable describing ourselves as "hippies" at that time. Certainly we adopted some of the attitudes prevalent at the time and espoused by our (mostly musical heroes). "Rural" and "self-sufficiency" are certainly concepts that were on the ascendant at the time. The bible for the times was the Whole Earth Catalog put together by Stewart Brand and a bunch of his cronies in Berkeley, California. Like anyone and everyone, we read about having "access to tools." The highlight of the month was the arrival in the mailbox of Mother Earth News.

We did not come to Vermont, however, to get back to the land. Nor were we highly aware of the Nearings and their role as modern-day Thoreaus at that time. We were in Vermont: (a) to avoid the traffic of metro New York, and (b) to find a place where people like us (long-haired, bearded folks) would be accepted—plus, it was a free place to stay! Our time at the Nearings' guest cottage led to a caretaking job on Lake Hortonia in central Vermont. Then came mud season—never a good time for making decisions in Vermont—and then came "The Call" from my father. He had a great opportunity for us to get the KaramelKorn concession at a mall he had developed in Fall River, Massachusetts. It would be our own business; he'd front the money; and we'd be on our way to making enough money to buy our own place in Vermont. The hippie dream.

Their literature gives me the creeps even today: "America's only one-stop source for everything you need to do caramel corn. . . . Fun foods to help you pave the way to profits. . . . Recession? Hell! Let's Sell. . . . We've got your personal bailout!"

For reasons that I still don't fully understand, we said yes. Clearly, this was a moment of weakness, if not a sign of early dementia.

Fall River and nearby New Bedford were known (at that time) as the armpits of New England. Aside from great Portuguese food, I found nothing in Fall River to enjoy. And living inside an enclosed mall really sucked.

Judy was pregnant. She became "with child" as soon as we got to Fall River. While the original idea was for us to run the store together, this became less and less practical. Once Zak was born, she took a smaller and smaller role in the store. Understandably. She was the lucky one.

I used to think that at least KaramelKorn had the virtue of tasting good when you were stoned. Before long, I was cured of that. I hated everything about it. I hated the smell. I hated the mall. I hated the customers. I hated my father. I hated myself.

My lesson learned was to never, NEVER do anything just for the money, because if the money isn't there, you've got nothing, or, as my grandparents would say, you've got "bupkis." First you have to do something that you like, and then figure out how to make it pay. It doesn't work the other way around.

Finally, I was so frustrated by my lot in life that I put up a sign: "Candy Apples — $0.25 each or 3 for $1.00." When most customers from then on ended up buying three for $1 (despite my ridiculing them) and business actually improved, I knew that my days in the "fun food" business were over. The strains of "We gotta get out of this place" welled up again. We packed the car and headed north, back to Vermont.

Lesson: About Beer

Alcohol has never been my drug of choice. I'm sure I've had my share of yellow, fizzy lagers over time, but American-style "corn lagers" have never held much appeal to me. Still don't. Bob Johnson introduced me to real beers. His house was the starting place for a lot of informal parties, both in my Seventh Generation days and after my exile from there. At his house, there were three faucets at the kitchen sink, one each for "hot and cold water—and one for the beer he made." That's where I was first exposed to good, hand-crafted beer.

Bob was the college buddy of one of my neighbors. I hired him to run the warehouse at Seventh Generation just before "the Perfect Storm" (see Chapter 7). Bob had some classical training as a French chef, and he did a stint as the cheesemaker at Shelburne Farms, the spectacular inn/restaurant/farm/sustainability center just south of Burlington. But why don't I turn the microphone over to Bob and let him tell his own story:

The Story of Bob

I brewed my first batch of beer in college. I actually brewed it in the bathtub. This was in 1978, before quality brewing ingredients were available, but there was a funky, little health-food store in Plainfield that sold cans of malt extract and dried-up hops. I can't say it was entirely successful.

After college, I moved to Baltimore and did an understudy in a classic French restaurant. This engaged me in the world of food and wine, but I wanted to move back to the North Country where I got a job as a cheesemaker at Shelburne Farms and spent two years making their award-winning cheddar.

After I had worked in the warehouse of Seventh Generation for over a year, I decided I needed a hobby. I found a homebrew bucket that someone had given me and said "Hmmm . . . maybe I'll try homebrewing again. I really threw myself into it, reading everything I could on brewing, both as an amateur hobbyist but also as a prospective professional.

I started homebrewing like a maniac. I learned whole grain brewing and eventually built a 10–12 gallon brewery. I quit my job at Seventh Generation, spent a summer cutting wood, and then decided that what I really wanted to do was to start a brewery. I took a job, unpaid, washing kegs at Otter Creek Brewing Company in Middlebury. Eventually they let me help out on the actual brewing process and offered me a job in distribution. The universe just kept delivering me these opportunities.

The Otter Creek people put me in touch with some folks looking to open a brewery in Martha's Vineyard, and I was considering moving down there when I ran into Alan on Church Street. He had been kicked out of Seventh Generation, and he asked me what I was doing. After I told him and he said "Well, if that doesn't work out, let's do a brewery in Burlington. I'm looking for a new business." I told him I would think about it.

Neither of us asked the most obvious question "Did Vermont, and specifically Burlington, need another craft brewer?" It's a good thing we didn't ask, because the answer was clearly "no."

Bob threw great parties with great food (and music), and I love parties with great food and music. Eventually I hired him to work at Seventh Generation as the warehouse manager. He did a great job, but as the company grew, so did his job responsibilities. This wasn't what he bargained for, however, so after a while he gave his notice and told us, "I'm going to go make great beer."

When he left, everyone at Seventh Generation wished him well. And I remember thinking, "Damn, I wish I had more time and money, 'cause it would be great to build a brewery for Bob to make his beer." The lesson here: be careful what you wish for.

After my forced exile from Seventh Generation, I was looking for the next opportunity. The way I remember it, I spent the entire summer barefoot, putting in a lot of time learning how to play the bass guitar. By now, I was both a confirmed entrepreneur and a card-carrying Vermonter.

Over the next few weeks, Bob taught me much about beer. I was a complete neophyte, but he educated me about malt, yeast, hops, and the magic that occurs when you mix them with water. Our enthusiasm mounted, although we were still groping about trying to figure out what would make us stand out in the marketplace. Those other Vermont brewers all made respectable brews.

The situation needed what in marketing lingo is called field research. We flew out to the Pacific Northwest, the hub of the craft-brewing universe, and set off on our own beer trek. We visited thirty-three breweries in eleven days. The market for craft beer out there was much more crowded, and some of the West Coast guys were approaching things very differently. Beer, for them, was a lifestyle, not a commodity beverage. In Vermont, at least from my non-technical perspective, all the brewers seemed cut from the same bolt of cloth, producing mostly English-style ales.

Earlier on our trip, we had met with an equipment salesman. He was beating us over the head with what we should and shouldn't do, and I asked a simple question, to which he replied, horrified, "You can't do that. Only the McMenamins do that!"

Bingo! (Music wells up in the background!)

I asked who the McMenamins were and where their nearest place was. Bob and I turned around then and there and made a beeline for the first (of many) McMenamins' pubs.

I was particularly impressed with the work of the McMenamin brothers, Mike and Brian. These two just don't fit the typical corporate mold, something I can relate to. Having first started in the pub business in 1974, Mike and a couple of his friends opened Portland's Produce Row Café. After a few years at Produce Row, Mike and his younger brother Brian opened their first brew pub, the Barley Mill Pub on S.E. Hawthorne, in 1983.

Two rules govern the McMenamins: First, it's got to be fun; and, second, if someone says you can't do it, that's a good place to start. They are both classic entrepreneurs and my kind of guys.

Mike and Brian graduated as political science majors at Oregon State University in Corvallis in the 1970s. Their advanced degrees came from visiting pubs and hostelries all around the world while on tour with the Dead (Grateful, that is). Of Irish descent and Portland birth, they have left an imprint on the culture (and architecture, as well as the taste buds) of Oregonians that rivals that of any of the legendary brewing families. At the time of our visit, Mike and Brian were developing the Edgefield Inn as kind of a hippie resort.

I realized that the McMenamins were doing beer as a lifestyle and a brand. Suddenly, it all connected with what Will Raap and Lyman Wood had taught me about connecting with customers. This was my "ah-ha!" moment. It all made sense. That was really the moment when Magic Hat was born. Even though beer is not a direct-marketing business, we could still make the same intimate connection with the customer if we marketed the company correctly. It doesn't have to be about beer. It can be about brand and lifestyle.

Did Vermont really need another craft brewery? If done the same as the others, with a geographic name and the same style beers, not really. But the McMenamin brothers showed me that there was another way—and that became the Magic Hat way.

Chapter 11
Focusing on the Wrong Things

With many good reasons not to go into the beer business, Bob and I go into the beer business. Lo and behold, we are instant successes, but you know that something has to happen, and it does. We become victims of our own success as we build a new brewery only to have the bank suddenly call the million-dollar loan that they gave us to build it.

Life: The Magic of the Hat

Seventh Generation was a once-in-a-lifetime rocket ship ride, both going up and going down, but Magic Hat was the more instructive experience from a business perspective.

Here are just a few reasons why I should never have been in the beer business:

1. I knew nothing about brewing beer.
2. I knew nothing about running a manufacturing business.
3. I had no contacts in the beverage business.
4. Vermont, and Burlington specifically, already had a number of excellent brewers.
5. Alcohol was never my drug of choice.
6. The distribution tier in the beer business is notoriously conservative, and I'm not.

7. My partner, Bob, had never been a professional brewer.

8. There was no transferability of my mail-order experience to beer.

9. There was no transferability of my reputation in the environment world to beer.

And the list goes on. Yet, here were Bob and I charging around the country, running up credit-card debt, blabbing our mouths about how we were starting a brewery. As a group, entrepreneurs are not known for their adherence to logic. That's why they occasionally accomplish the impossible. If you really want to light a fire under an entrepreneur, tell him that something cannot be done. They'll do it, just to prove you wrong.

What was I thinking? And yet, when the dust cleared some seventeen years later, Magic Hat was one of the largest craft breweries in the country, and still growing when the beer industry, overall, was flat to declining.

Let the record show that Magic Hat retained its status as an independent brewer (who knew, at the time, that it would be "just barely") after even the "King of Beers," Budweiser, had succumbed.

Bob and I hooked up in the spring of 1993. This was not to be an equal partnership; I had learned that lesson. I would be the final decision-maker, although I happily deferred to Bob on product and equipment issues. In May we made our mini-epic journey to the West Coast, visiting 33 breweries in 11 days. We returned to Vermont fully energized and started to write a business plan and look for space while trying to raise money.

We had a name; and, thanks to the inspiration of the McMenamins, we had at least the rough idea of a brand position. And we had a plan. Magic Hat would be a draft-only facility, with initial distribution in the greater Burlington area.

The brand I wanted to create for Magic Hat would be

entertaining—steeped in mystery and surprise, waiting for people to discover the hidden messages—and intended for night consumption (rather than for drinking while mowing lawns and going to baseball games). It would be consistent and authentic. Apple, BMW—these are great brands that have been carefully managed (and protected) over the years. Businesses can have a point of view that extends to its customers. This is a message I first fully understood from the lessons of Lyman Wood, Will Raap, and Marshall Thurber.

(A good book on the subject of branding is Onward by Howard Schultz, chairman and C.E.O. of Starbucks. It shows what can happen when a brand starts to slip and how one can go back to the basics of the brand in order to right the ship.)

Here's another comment on our brand positioning that I found interesting, from Josh Patrick, the principal of Stage 2 Planning Partners and a long-time friend, who has always maintained that the "magic" in Magic Hat was not about beer, but about fashion: "Alan figured out what drives a microbrewery business. It's more fashion than beer. He's built a brand based on it being cool, and fashion is about being cool. It's not about being the best beer in the world. He gets a buzz going about his beer. He's no more cool than a gazillion other people. It's that he's attracted people who want to be around a cool product. Ben & Jerry's did that, too. It was just ice cream, but they made it fashion. Building a brand is so hard, and Alan's done it a couple of times. I don't think he could explain how it's done, but he's really, really good at it."

The connection between Magic Hat and the arts was entirely intentional. I've always felt that when you give back to the community, you create a feedback loop in which the community gives back in the form of support. We decided that our focus would be the arts, because I always wanted to be in the music business, and many of my friends are musicians and artists. I don't have much in the way of musical talent, so here was my chance.

In the summer of 1993 we developed the recipe for a Red Ale that we dubbed "Bob's First Ale." We did about a dozen test brews that summer. Now all we needed was a brewery.

We set a goal to get the beer to market at the first Blues Cabaret, a festival of blues, to be held at Memorial Auditorium in Burlington in February 1994. We were buying brewing equipment from Alan Pugsley, a partner in Shipyard Brewing Company in Kennebunkport. He agreed to let Bob come in and brew one batch per week using their equipment. This made for pretty hairy war stories about shuttling back and forth to Maine. Initially, we'd hook up a U-Haul trailer to my old Mercedes diesel (it had 285,000 miles on the odometer). Bob would haul empty kegs to Maine and come back with full ones. One time, he and a friend actually delivered eleven kegs in Bob's Volkswagen Jetta. They even survived being stopped by the police for a safety check! Necessity is the mother of invention.

We were making and selling fifteen kegs a week, which in our minds was a lot of beer, but it was less than what the demand was in the market. In April 1994, Shipyard opened a new brewery in Portland, Maine and wasn't using it to full capacity. One day, as we were constructing our little draft-only brewery, I got a call from Pugsley saying, "You know, we can do bottled beer for you, too."

There were several reasons we had decided to limit the original brewery to draft beer only, some related to product quality, but frankly, it was far more related to the fact that installing a bottling line is a major investment, a much bigger bite than we were willing to take on. But bottled beer without needing an investment? That's an offer too good to refuse.

I remember getting our first case from Shipyard a few months later. We had just hired our first real employee, Stacey Steinmetz (as a sales rep), who took a sip and said, "Man, have you ever tasted a better beer?"

Bob, ever the perfectionist, could detect minute quality variations, but even he was impressed: "In retrospect I could have improved the process, but Shipyard really did a good job, and seeing a bottle with a label on it was cool. Every once in a while, I'll be in a bar or at the supermarket and I'll see someone with a bottle of Magic Hat—you can't take that for granted. In your head you're screaming 'That's my beer! And they're buying it!' It's a total rush."

And the bottles just evaporated. Stacey, Bob, or I would go into a store that was supposed to be carrying our product, and there would be none. Then we'd get on the phone with the distributor who'd sputter, "But I just dropped off ten cases yesterday," and we'd discover that they had sold out.

We were totally locked in on running the business, but everything was new and therefore difficult. Entropy reigned! It's hard to create order out of chaos. There was no structure. There was no system. There was no nothing.

Stacey had come on board our feast of fools in August 1994. I had met her when she did an internship at Seventh Generation. After an abortive stint in corporate America in St. Louis, she wanted to come back to Burlington (she was a University of Vermont grad) and called me every few weeks to see what we had for her. We hired her to be our first brewery representative, but really she was our first all-everything.

I was still on a steep learning curve about the product and the business. We found an old brick building on Flynn Avenue in Burlington and started making decisions about equipment, yeast, and the brand. Meanwhile, the credit-card debt was rising. I told Bob, "Don't worry! We'll figure something out." It was a time filled with positive energy and unbridled hope for the future.

We officially opened our doors in November 1994. Stacey literally had to create the company's office there by scrubbing down the old brick, then waterproofing and sealing it before the carpet could be laid. We brewed our first batch, of fifteen barrels, that Thanksgiving.

It fell to Stacey to browbeat accounts into taking our beer. That's not easy when the competition is Anheuser-Busch and Molson. Here's how she remembers it: "We didn't have a lot of money to promote the beer, so we tried to sell accounts on the romance of the small, local thing. They'd respond by saying 'That's great, but Molson was here last night and gave out three cases of T-shirts and four cases of hats.' We couldn't do that with our T-shirts. We had to make them last. They disappeared way too fast."

But there was also the palpable sense of something happening. Remember those "calls" I talked about? First, it was Peter Demuth calling to lock up my Seventh Generation shares. Then it was a beer distributor from Maryland whose daughter, a student at UVM, had brought home a case of Magic Hat for Christmas vacation, and he wanted to distribute the beer in Maryland.

We doubled our capacity to 30 kegs a week, then 60, then 120. Even though we made our share of mistakes, it was exciting because whatever we did was successful. There was no such thing as failure. I was a genius once again. We were always a sales-driven organization with people clamoring for more of our beer than we could produce. There wasn't time for much more in life than making beer, selling beer, and making sure we had enough money.

This was entrepreneur heaven!

Not that it was real heaven. "We were always wet," remembers Bob. "On Flynn Avenue, you were wet and cold the entire time. Everything happened in the refrigeration room, so at any given time you could have one person transferring beer from the fermentation room to the conditioning tanks while someone else was filtering beer, another kegging, another shipping. The kegs were three or four deep with hoses everywhere. You were constantly breaking your knuckles because there was no room to move."

And then there was our fermentation room. We were using a yeast that fermented in open-top tanks—highly unusual in the U.S., but very popular in England. To protect the yeast, we needed a separate fermentation room. When beer ferments, it gives off HUGE amounts of CO_2. Bob kept telling me about this, and how we needed special venting in the fermentation room to get the CO_2 out. But our budget just didn't have room for sophisticated air-handling equipment, so we would just have to do without. I didn't fully understand why one needed this equipment until I went into the fermentation room early one day and almost passed out from the CO_2. How in the world could people work in that room? What if someone fell into a tank?

Here's one of our original brewers on the joys of the fermentation room:

Matt Zambarano on Magic Hat's Fermentation Room:

The alchemy of fermentation may conjure up all sorts of mystical thoughts for some, but for me, it's carbon dioxide! Have you ever been in a completely unvented fermentation room with no windows? I have. Many times. At 5 a.m., with no one else in the building. Nobody to find me dead for hours. No joke.

Open fermentation in an ale brewery is an amazing thing of beauty, but holy crap, it's dangerous! I would show up at 5 a.m., open the side door to the brewery, and turn the lights on. I could instantly smell the yeast explosion that had taken place overnight in the fermentation room, and already feel the CO_2 in my lungs. First order of business: check the temperature of the fermenting beer. In order to do that, you had to enter the fermentation room and check the temps on the tanks. How do you do this in a room with little oxygen? Well, you take a really deep breath and run in.

Have you ever wondered if CO_2 burns your eyes? It does. I was really good at checking temps and taking samples really quickly. If there were two of us there, one would make the mad dash in, and the other would heckle the whole time.

At one point it dawned on me that brewing beer was not unlike being a dairy farmer. There was no such thing as nights or weekends off. You make a batch of beer and it goes through the process, and you can't say, "Oh, I'm not going to pitch the yeast because today is Sunday." You do what you have to do when you have to do it. The cows need to be milked, and they don't care if it's Christmas or Thanksgiving or someone's birthday or 3 in the morning. When beer needs to be racked, it needs to be racked. When yeast needs to be cropped, it needs to be cropped, and the yeast doesn't care if it's Sunday afternoon.

Everything, and everyone, was jamming.

We were a success, albeit on a small scale, from day one. More important, coming to work was fun again. While there were plenty of causes for stress, as there are in any start-up business, I felt that at least I was back in control of my own life. I was back behind the wheel!

Part of what we wanted to do with Magic Hat was to bring a little theater to the beer-drinking experience. We had a variety of ways of achieving this—sponsoring concerts and events, staging on premise promotions, but also through our own Artifactory visitor center.

We talk about "putting a performance into every bottle" and

the place to do that is in an environment that you can control. For us, that meant the brewery. While jazz festivals and karaoke contests are wonderful, the stars of the show are the performers on stage. Beer may be an integral part of the experience, but only in a supporting role. The Artifactory gave us our own stage. And, eventually, we held some epic parties at/in the brewery itself

People started showing up at the door wanting to see the brewery. This is a pain in the ass, but it's how you create brand loyalty. We started selling growlers of Bob's First Ale and Magic Hat T-shirts, but people wanted anything with "Magic Hat" written on it. People even stole our signs. Whenever we could, we would give informal but intimate brewery tours. You'd be stepping over hoses and tasting malt from the bins. There were always a couple of employee dogs wandering around, adding to the home-brewed atmosphere.

Beer drinkers are a curiously loyal lot. One of my earliest beer memories was hearing how fanatical beer drinkers would go to insane lengths to score some Coors Beer, which was then available only in the Rocky Mountain states. Beer drinkers like to visit breweries. And they like to buy stuff associated with their beer. They'll show up, unannounced, anyway, so you may as well accommodate them and provide them with a memorable experience. Hence the Artifactory, a place where our growing community could gather together, test new beers, and be immersed in the Magic Hat culture.

Cool stuff and an interesting factory tour have always been part of the Magic Hat brand. It's also a part of the experience that I enjoy. I definitely considered it a significant part of my job to wander out to the Artifactory and to serve some samples to customers. This was my house and my guests—not at all like selling KaramelKorn to the glazed people at the mall.

The Artifactory has also been the site of more than one after-hours parties. It was at one of these that a woman, who turned out to be some kind of heiress, approached me and said, out of the blue, "I like what you're doing. I'd like to invest some money in your company."

That's the way things fell into place for the first few years of Magic Hat. We were brewing as much as we could and selling everything we could make. We were in the bottled beer business without investing a penny. Money was always tight, but when we needed some, an heiress would show up, or the phone would ring and it would be the lawyer for Seventh Generation, offering to buy my shares that had been worthless just the day before.

We were always able to pull out a rabbit from the magic hat.

Lesson: The Tale of the Tap Knob

Quick, tell me everything you know about tap knobs. If you are like most mortals, or like me before I became involved in the beer business, you would know this about tap knobs:

1. They are what the bar tender pulls to dispense draft beer.

2. They identify the specific type or brand of beer.

If you are a tap knob aficionado, you might also note the following about tap knobs:

1. They are about 12 inches high.

2. They are given to the bar or tavern by the distributor.

3. They are generally made of plastic, or plastic made to look like wood.

If you are "in the biz," then you probably also know that the average tap knob costs about $12 to $15 to manufacture and that the brewer (generally) picks up the tab for tap knobs.

Then, there's the Magic Hat tap knob. It was not in our DNA to take the proven path, so we decided to reinvent the tap knob. There was a rationale for this. There are relatively few ways for brewers to establish their brand at the point of purchase in a bar, and they are: coasters, napkins, table tents, and tap knobs. The first three are cheesy and disposable, sometimes there for the customer to see, but frequently not. The tap knob, however, makes a statement and is always present.

We designed our original tap knob to be 17 inches high. It had a wrought-iron shaft topped with a clear ball of hand-blown glass that was wrapped with some custom lettering to identify us. It looks more like a sorcerer's staff than a tap knob. It also required us to work with four separate vendors and weighed in at a final cost to us of around $60. Anybody in the beer business will tell you this is nuts. Including me.

Complicating things further, the sales people who work for beer distributors are accustomed to throwing the tap knobs into their trunks and forgetting about them until the next stop. Guess what happens when you throw a custom-blown glass ball into the trunk? Crash, tinkle. Also, guess what happens behind the bar when your tap knobs are all the same except for this one, which is exotic, sensual, and taller than the rest? People can't resist giving it a little tug, and little tugs can add up to a lot of wasted beer.

So the Magic Hat tap knob was a disaster, right?

It was a huge success! For a mere $60, we had a fixture at the point of purchase that screamed "quality and distinction." Put those two attributes together and you get "cool," and that's what Magic Hat was all about. As the years passed and we developed new products—#9, Circus Boy, Vinyl—we always tried to keep in mind that our point-of-purchase materials had to be highly visual, theatrical, irreverent, and therefore distinctive.

We were fanatics about this.

A side benefit to this is that our tap knobs became gift items that we sold in the Artifactory, and they continue to be highly prized among collectors of breweriana (sometimes called "beeraphenalia"). If you don't believe me, just check on eBay.

And . . . back to Life:

Another critical part of our success was our (own) sales force. When we were starting the business and I knew nothing, I figured I should learn from the best—who, at that time were Sam Adams (on the craft side) and Anheuser Busch (now owned by Inbev, and called ABI). I looked at both companies and noticed that each had its own sales forces. It was pretty much unheard of at that time for a small craft brewery to employ (and pay for) its own sales force, instead of counting on the distributor's sales team to sell our beer. At that time, I really didn't understand the significance of this, but figured that if the two best beer companies were doing it, it had to be smart, because why would these companies be paying their own people to do this if it were not necessary?

Early on, I took massive amounts of ridicule from my fellow brewery owners for having our own sales force. "You really need your own people in order to sell your beer?" I heard this constantly, with the implicit message being, "Our beer is so good it sells itself—why can't yours?" But after two or three years, the ridicule stopped and the calls started coming in from everybody who had made fun of me: "How do you structure your sales force?" "How do you compensate them?" "How do you measure their productivity?"

Having our own sales force set us apart and really fueled our growth, especially as we started selling our beer in other states and relied on our sales people to manage our distributors there, to make sure that we were getting a disproportionate amount of mind share (compared to the other brands), telling our story to customers one beer at a time.

Chapter 12
Getting Real

We take a crash course in reality, as our only route to survival is being very, very good at what we do. And what we do is to run a very tight business while developing a brand that is achieving cult status within the craft-brewing world. The bank loan is replaced by private financing, but we trade one set of financial challenges for another. Somehow we keep brewing, keep growing, keep entering new markets, and keep meeting payroll. Along the way, I have to fire Bob and bring in professional management.

Lesson: Your Friendly Banker

By 1995 we had achieved the Holy Grail of business start-ups—profitability. And by 1997, we maxed out the capacity of our Flynn Avenue brewery. Luckily, we had some capacity elasticity due to our relationship with Shipyard.

While Bob was handling the brewing side, the really hard work took place in the bars and taverns, late at night. Stacey was doing a bang-up job in Vermont, but the beer was beginning to spill beyond the state borders. Mike Brown signed on to help us build the brand in other New England states. As he remembers, it wasn't easy: "I'd done a lot of home brewing with Bob, and during the testing of the sample brews I'd spent a lot of time talking sales and marketing over a couple of beers. I was really just a friend watching these two guys put a brewery together and getting a buzz started. I was hired in February 1995 to manage the sales effort, but Stacey didn't need a lot of managing, so I directed my efforts to supporting our new distributors in western Massachusetts and Connecticut. I had the job that any twenty-two-year-old would die for, walking up to tables of guys chugging beers and smoking cigarettes, and slapping stickers on their chests. Unfortunately, I was thirty-five at this time. I'd spend eight to ten hours during the day with distributors, then five hours at night putting stickers on drunks in smoky bars. The only thing that made it worth it was the positive reinforcement about the brand. Without that, it wouldn't have been worth it."

We decided to come out with a summer wheat beer, but like everything Magic Hat, it couldn't be just another wheat beer. Bob came up with a good formula, but we needed a good name. One of our brewers was in a bar one night when the rep from another brewery was holding court. Someone asked him about Magic Hat, and he said, dismissively, "Oh, that hocus-pocus company." Our brewer reported this to us, and Bob and I looked at each other with the same thought. We now had the name for our new beer—Hocus-Pocus. My favorite naming story ever!

Grimaldi was a one-off beer that we produced for the Burlington Beer Festival in 1996. It was a pineapple beer. Bob hated it: "Grimaldi is a skeleton in my closet. I don't like to talk about it. They put a gun to my head and made me do it. It was named after Michael Grimaldi, who wanted us to send him to Hawaii to distribute our beers. He wanted us to do a coconut beer, too. But, you know, people still ask for that pineapple beer."

Even our mistakes were successful.

Jinx was the name of our fall seasonal. Bob used Scottish peat-smoked malt to make a beer that was both highly alcoholic and complex as hell, unlike any other beer out there. I wanted to call it Mother, because I could picture people walking into bars and saying, "I'll have a Mother." Unfortunately, the Whistler Brewing Company had already used the name (duh!), but Jinx was a great name, too.

Then, the shit hit the fan. This time, it wasn't the market crashing or the U.S. invading Iraq. This time it was Miller Brewing Company buying Shipyard to establish a beachhead in the craft-brewing market.

I got the news one summer morning when I was in Maine to discuss renewing the contract for our bottled beer. This was a stunner. I could imagine someone at Miller suddenly waking up and saying, "So . . . why is it we're brewing beer for a competitor?"

Miller is one of the Milwaukee breweries started by German immigrants in the mid-1800s. A little more than a century later, they were already part of the massive industry consolidation that, in my opinion, created the void that the craft brewers filled. At that time, they were a division of tobacco giant Phillip Morris. Subsequently, they were acquired by SAB Breweries of South Africa, then merged with Molson and Coors to create a new conglomerate, MillerCoors. (Are you following this? Musical chairs has always been part of the beer industry, and continues to this day.)

I'll never fully understand their motivations for acquiring Shipyard, but what was crystal clear to Bob and me back in 1997 is that our cozy deal with a reliable partner for bottled beer was now in jeopardy. By now we were highly dependent on sales of our bottled beer. If they decided to stop supplying us, we would be (I think this is the right business term) shit out of luck.

We met with the Miller people, who assured us that the status quo would be maintained. I countered by insisting they post a $5 million dollar bond, payable immediately if they decided to break their contract. We could then use the bond payment to build a bottling facility. They, in turn, responded with a laugh. They were not going to be pushed around by a tiny brewery in Vermont. Bob and I, in consultation with other Magic Hat investors, decided that we had to investigate other options, including building a new brewery with a bottling line.

Looking back, I'd say we were a little cocky, but why not? We were hearing nothing but raves about the beer. We were operating at full capacity (and then some). And we were playing with the big dogs and not letting ourselves get pushed around by them. We decided to talk to a few banks to float the idea of building a new brewery. Lesson here: never believe your own press clippings.

As part of the process of writing this book I asked my friend and long-time financial advisor Ross Anderson to contribute a few words on banks and bankers. Here's what he has to say.

Ross Anderson on Important Things To Understand About Bankers

Alan and I met at a meeting of some crazy, not-so-laid back entrepreneurs called the Mountain Group sometime in the late 1980s. I was in the automobile business, with dealerships in Vermont, and for reasons that were never fully explained, had been invited to join this esoteric group of bright, outside-the-box business types. All kinds of businesses were represented—gardener, ice-cream maker, film producer, record company executive, fashion designer, retailer, restaurateur. But auto dealer? It goes to show that in Vermont anything is possible.

Automobile dealers, of necessity, have tremendous experience dealing with the banking profession as borrowers, placers of financial instruments, and managers of cash flow. Our industry is hardly the only small, rapidly expanding, and cash-poor business to be involved with a bank. Many different types of business structures need access to capital, and the glue that helps all of us keep operating day-to-day is the bank.

The personality, drives, and goals of an entrepreneur are diametrically opposed to those of a banker. Entrepreneurs are risk takers; bankers are not! (This does not count the mega-bankers of recent bailouts who are willing to take huge risks as long as it's with your money, not theirs.)

When I met Alan, he had left Seventh Generation and had started Magic Hat, cooking up strange and magical brews with Bob Johnson. After creating enough mystical concoctions, they decided to join forces and to create a brand. More accurately, Bob just wanted to brew while Alan had visions of a great national brand ricocheting inside his creative skull.

Alan, ever looking for capital, suggested that since I was in the process of selling my dealerships to a couple of our employees, I invest in this new company. I was very protective of my funds and said I was interested, but only if I became a member of the board. There was silence from Alan, followed by a chuckle, and finally a loud guffaw. Alan suddenly realized that getting capital from an individual was tantamount to getting funding from a bank. They won't give it to you unless you've got it! Get it?

A few observations about bankers:

1. They pick up deposits, but not checks. You will go broke taking them to lunch.

2. It's easy to borrow when you have some capital or a sugar daddy.

3. The minute things get shaky, they run for cover quicker than a rabbit.

4. Don't do business with a bank that has a competitor on its board.

5. Borrow much more than you need. You'll need it, and they won't usually come in for a second round just because you've grown a bit and are shy some capital.

6. When your local bank (do these exist anymore?) gets sold, start shopping for the next one immediately.

7. When someone from the bank's home office "wants to meet," you know you are on the way to meet their "workout team"!

8. Bankers are not your friend.

A small business is always chasing money to become a bigger business. As a result, the creator of a business—like a politician—spends an inordinate amount of time chasing money when time would be better spent building the brand. However, a small business cannot afford to hire someone to chase money, so it falls on the creator and members of the board.

While Magic Hat was still in the small brewery stage, the company was able to scratch enough capital from friends, believers, and a local bank to grow to the stage where they needed a much larger facility. We were all excited to be part of this venture. The opening of the new brewery was a hoot! Judy Newman decided that we needed the proper *feng shui* (the Chinese practice of orienting buildings in harmony with local features such as bodies of water, stars, or compass directions). We all held hands in a great circle and did our thing. However, our new landlord (whose hand I was holding) and our local banker (on the other side of the circle) did not seem quite as enthusiastic. Lesson learned: never invite straight arrows who have no sense of humor to quirky openings! They may control your future.

It's no surprise that it didn't take long for Magic Hat to hit a few bumps. We hadn't raised the capital needed to support the expansion, and then our local bank got sold to a large regional/semi-national from the Midwest. The manure hit the fan, and we very quickly were "out of compliance" with their lending criteria. This gave us the distinct pleasure of meeting their regional "workout team" with their "We are here to help you" mantra.

In fairness, we did need some help, and their loans could have been in jeopardy, as we were a growing business still unable to keep up with the demand for the product. We would make it over the top, if only they would re-negotiate our terms and pour in a few more bucks. The meetings were tough, stressful, and humorous if you had a quirky sense of humor.

Luckily, if there is a long suit for Alan Newman, it's a quirky sense of humor. We needed it!

Shopping to secure financing for our new brewery we half expected to be tossed out on our ears when we visited our first bank. On the contrary, the first bank we talked to was quite solicitous. So was the second—and the third. Not only did they all seem to think we had a viable proposition, but they started to make us offers for loan deals that seemed too good to be true. Maybe we weren't just a group of crazy hippies making beer, after all. The guys in suits seemed to think we were for real. How could such serious guys be wrong?

The decision to build a new brewery was now made. We found a property on Bartlett Bay Road in South Burlington. It was a former Grossman's Lumber Yard with none of the romance and charm of the red brick brewery on Flynn Avenue. We knew we could use some of our house magic to tart it up. It was also just up the road from a municipal sewage treatment plant that was designed by John Todd as a "living machine."

John is a Canadian-born biologist who specializes in ecological design; he is a professor at the University of Vermont, the founder of the New Alchemy Institute and does research into applications that become the basis of alternative technologies. His principal professional interests have included solving problems of food production and waste-water processing through an integrated process known as a "living machine."

He is as close to being a real-life alchemist as exists in the world. Somehow it seemed right that there would be a living machine right down the road from our new brewery. After all, weren't we alchemists, too, turning water, grain, and hops into sparkling, delicious beer via the magic of yeast? I had visions of having Magic Hat's waste products being treated in a greenhouse full of plants, fish, and water—and turning it into a local "butterfly ranch" tourist attraction. Unfortunately, it never was to be.

My initial inclination had been to raise private equity to finance the construction and equipment we needed, but the offers we were getting from the banks were too good to be true. Key Bank made an especially attractive offer, lending us $1.2 million on very favorable terms. We took the money and started building like crazy. Construction started in May or June of 1997 and by October, Magic Hat was flowing.

There was a significant moment when we broke ground (referred to earlier by Ross). Mike Brown also remembers it: "We had a cleansing ceremony, a spiritual gathering to invite good spirits to be present and to reflect and say thank you. There was nothing there aside from a bunch of swallow shit. We stood in a circle and paid respect to the forces of the Earth, fire, water, and air. The moment sticks out as one of the few where we could sit and ponder, one of the few moments when we actually stood still. We knew we were taking a big step."

The long-story-short is that just a year later, we received a letter dated September 28, 1998, demanding payment in full—$1.157 million—within ten days! Unfortunately, I was a tad short (roughly by $1.157 million). This became the bullet that, twelve years later, killed Magic Hat. I framed the letter and still have it.

Even now, I'm still occasionally asked the question, "If you had it all to do over again, would you have done the bank deal?" My standard answer is: "DO I LOOK LIKE AN IDIOT?" No offense to the mentally challenged, but the benefit of hindsight is what makes this look like a blunder. Given the circumstances and information at the time, I think we made the right decision. We were still growing like crazy, 20 to 30 percent a year. Chasing down investment capital is a time-intensive task and involves staging countless dog-and-pony shows and factory tours. It's not the best use of an entrepreneur's time.

Ironically, some years later we received a letter informing us that we were to be awarded the prestigious 5x5x5 Award from Vermont Business Magazine, sponsored by (you guessed it!) Key Bank. Knowing that I would undoubtedly say something that I would later regret, I had to send someone else to the award ceremony in my place. Bankers had now joined doctors and KaramelKorn kustomers on my "least favorite people" list.

Key Bank, it turns out, had been acquired by a larger bank from the Midwest. Suddenly, and inexplicably, the rules for loans had changed. However, no one had bothered to tell us.

Life: The Beer Flows On

Bob supervised the construction of the new brewery, and even though he was now in way over his head (as all of us were), things went great and we finished relatively on time and on budget. The first few months of operation, however, were chaotic. Chaos is fine with me, because I don't need much structure, but the rest of the world does.

We started missing deadlines. It was ugly and painful. Everyone wanted to quit. The learning curve was incredibly steep. In essence we were taking people from an overgrown home brewery, which is what Flynn Avenue was, and putting them into a factory. At the end of most days, Bob, Mike, and Stacey would come to me and beat me up with, "We need management—someone like Steve Hood!" Steve had been our operations manager at Seventh Generation, taming very similar problems during our fast growth period. After about the fifteenth time I heard this, I said, "I have a great idea—let's get Steve Hood back." We needed some management desperately.

Enter Steve Hood . . . in his own words

The barking dog chasing the pickup truck has just caught up with it, so to speak. Now what?

I arrived in the summer of 1997. The brewery on Bartlett Bay Road was becoming a reality and would be ready to open, on time, and damn close to being on budget. It was time to make the beer and move ahead to a bright future. And sales were strong.

The team was smart, hardworking, and dedicated, and had the experience to bring the brand into focus and into the marketplace. Bob— brewing and product development; Mike—sales; Stacey—marketing and sales; and Alan—all of the above.

Now they had a brand-new 37,000 square feet of brewery, a spiffy Krones bottling line, a JVNW 50 bbl brewhouse, 50 and 100 bbl stainless tanks, and all the space they needed. The future was bright.

When I met with Bob, Mike, and Alan just then, it was clear that the challenges that came with the transition from a small draft brewery and sales-and-marketing organization to a by-God manufacturing operation were real, and the growing pains were severe and at some points life-threatening for the business.

Here's the short list of problems we faced:

- Bob led the small brewing team through the commissioning and start-up of a brew house that was larger and more sophisticated than anything that they'd had experience with. It consumed them, leaving the balance of the operation to bring on line.

- Waste water (the high-strength waste that is the challenge and responsibility of every brewery), became a life-threatening variable when the local permit issued by the state was withdrawn immediately after the commissioning of the brewery. Bob had to become a wastewater expert in a very short time, and to come up with low-cost, creative, best-practices solutions.

- At the same time, Bob had primary responsibility for bringing the new (Krones) bottling line up to speed, getting all of that good Magic Hat beer into bottles and cases, something he/we had no experience with.

- Six-packs and cases had to be made to feed that Krones line, a task that required LOTS of people (until years later when these processes were automated). There was no dedicated H.R. person, and managing the people issues introduced a new level of complexity for the small team of managers.

- Draft production ran ahead of keg supplies, and while the brewhouse and bottling line were still in the process of getting up and running, empty kegs were being unloaded from trucks on the dock, cleaned and refilled, and sometimes reloaded onto the same truck. Normally, kegs would be returned to the brewery and be replaced with full ones. In this case, however, there was no inventory of full kegs, so the truck would wait while the empty kegs for that account were refilled. The brewery was not keeping up with demand. The shipping and receiving processes in this large new space were close to non-existent and it was a sign of the times that getting the trash out was beyond our capabilities. This turned into a shorthand way of saying that we were in over our heads, and became a daily refrain: "If we could just get the garbage out, everything will be ok."

▸ At the same time, while day-to-day shop-floor operations were struggling to get to their feet, the "back shop" systems were breaking down—i.e., the basic systems for order processing, production planning, materials supply, and inventory control, which had outlived their useful lives.

▸ Finally, the accounting systems that were adequate for the small business couldn't keep up with the expansion, resulting in no visibility with inventories, inadequate control of work-in-process, and delayed monthly financial information and reporting. When information was available, it painted a bleak picture, with overheads significantly higher than projected in the pro-formas, and a business model that wasn't sustainable. The business wouldn't be viable if costs weren't brought into line—immediately.

Bottom line—the "relevant range" for the people, systems and processes had been outgrown. What had worked in the small, hands-on draft brewery simply couldn't keep up and almost everything, from team to process, had to be re-thought, and re-designed, fast.

The small team of skilled, hard-working, smart and completely dedicated people were in the deep end of the pool and swimming hard. Some decided that this new animal wasn't for them and moved on. The rest (most) worked hard, learned, adapted, and led the business on to a strong brand and business.

But in that moment in 1997, the dream had come true and the dog was behind the wheel of the pickup truck now.

Life: The Silver Lining

There was a silver lining of sorts. Admittedly, Magic Hat was out of control. This isn't unusual for a young company that's growing quickly. You are almost always in uncharted territory. Building a brewery? Me? Bob came from the craft side of the business. He had never installed a bottling line. Having a pile of money can exacerbate (and exasperate!) the situation, because you are giving inexperienced people the shovels to dig their holes faster. Paul Hawken, author and founder of Smith & Hawken, points out that as many companies have collapsed by having too much money as not enough.

I experienced this firsthand at Seventh Generation. Jeffrey went out to raise a million dollars and came back with three million. We were in the mode of responding quickly to opportunity and maintaining our leadership. If a situation could be solved by throwing money at the wall, we threw money. A dozen businesses could have been started with the cash we burned through in those early years at Seventh Generation.

There was no cash to burn at Magic Hat. Virtually overnight, we had to learn to be frugal and low-to-the-ground. We were in a perpetual stage of being stretched too thin. We lived this way for the next dozen years. There was no choice. We solved problems with creativity, not with cash.

I'm probably better known for my crazy glasses, outrageous Mardi Gras costumes, and off-the-wall marketing schemes, but I took a crash course in something with the very sexy name of "capacity utilization." I'm not an economist, but, simply stated, capacity utilization is the relationship between what you are actually producing and what you are theoretically capable of producing. The ideal percentage of actual to theoretical varies from industry to industry.

At our Flynn St. brewery we were actually over 100 percent capacity. Despite what you might think, this is not good, because it usually means that you are doing crazy (and unnecessarily expensive things) to meet demand. You might be paying excessive overtime, incurring premium shipping charges, running an unprofitable third shift, avoiding required maintenance—the causes are infinite, but the effects are all costly and stress-inducing.

Having too low a capacity utilization, however, is even more damaging. In manufacturing, you have fixed costs and variable costs. Fixed costs (taxes, payments on equipment, heat, electricity) are the same from month to month whether you brew one barrel of beer or a million barrels. Variable costs (product ingredients, labor, commissions, marketing expenses) rise and fall with the output. To some extent, these are the result of product demand, but there's a certain degree to which you can control variable expenses. The good companies are the ones that manage this part of the business process very well.

The sweet spot in the brewing business is supposedly in the 80 to 85 percent range of capacity utilization. This is achievable when you're a company like Budweiser, Miller, and Coors that's been brewing beer for more than a hundred years, and have a significant history in measuring and managing the demand for your product. And your year-to-year business is either flat or growing slowly. It's nearly impossible, however, when you are a small, inexperienced craft brewery suddenly dealing with an explosive demand for your product and you're run by a bunch of old hippies who are very good at whipping up excitement about the brand, but less good at managing the details of a manufacturing business (which is really what the beer-brewing business is).

When we began brewing at the Bartlett Bay Road brewery, our capacity utilization was at—gulp!—10 percent. We had built for the future, but suddenly the future was now. There wasn't a lot we could do about our fixed costs, so we had to become experts at managing the variable costs—a task made even more challenging by the fact that beer is a highly perishable product. Forget all the hype you've heard about Beechwood Aging, beer is at its best the moment it leaves the brewery. From there, it is all downhill. Quality control, especially for a craft brewer, has to be extremely high. You can't afford to have old product out there; beer drinkers are too sensitive and too fickle. One bad batch and you are a goner.

I don't know if we knew the phrase "just-in-time" manufacturing back in the '90s, but we certainly had grasped the concept by this time. We couldn't afford to keep inventory of either raw ingredients or finished product. It had to get in and out in a hurry. We became very adept at coordinating the sales and manufacturing cycles so that they were tightly coordinated. We told our distributors to tell us what they needed and when, and that we'd get it to them, but not to expect to phone us with an order and have us deliver a truckload at a moment's notice.

Capital Chasing Capacity

Fritz Maytag, part of the Maytag appliance family, is one of the grandfathers of the craft beer resurgence. He bought the little Anchor Steam brewery in San Francisco out of bankruptcy in 1974 and turned it into a national success. At a conference early in my beer career (but unfortunately not early enough), Fritz explained that the cash needed to grow a manufacturing business was not the same as a smooth growth curve, but occurs in "steps."

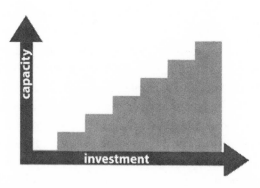

In many businesses there is a straight-line relationship between investment and capacity. Not so in brewing. First, you must invest in capacity, then you ride that investment until you fill that capacity. Eventually, assuming all goes well, you exceed capacity, necessitating another round of investment where capital is needed for additional growth. If your company is growing at 25 to 30 percent a year (as it is for many craft brewing start-ups), these steps come frequently. Sounds simple, but not understanding this simple principle caused years of pain and suffering at Magic Hat.

One of the problems with industry standards such as the rule about 80 to 85 percent capacity utilization is that although the standards may be valid, you never know exactly where you are in a fast-moving environment, which it always was at Magic Hat. As a result, you tend to toggle instantly from the problems of being under capacity to those of being over capacity.

When you are at 10 percent capacity, you'd better grow at warp speed. When you are at 120 percent, you'd better expand fast. There's no looking back—no taking a deep breath and saying, "Let's just slow things down for a while." You're walking over hot coals, and if you stop in your tracks, you're going to be smelling burning flesh pretty damn quickly.

Dudley Davis, the Last of the Local Bankers

Hard as this may be to believe, there was a day when local banks lent money to business owners looking to start or expand their businesses. And, even harder to believe, these deals were often done with a handshake, rather than today's deals (venture capital/private equity) that require three reams of paper and $100,000 in legal fees.

Here in Burlington, there was just such a man—and such a bank—when I was starting my entrepreneurial career: Dudley Davis at the Merchants Bank (which is aptly named).

I never met the man or ever did business with him, but so many of my fellow businesspeople in Vermont speak glowingly of him that he deserves a shout-out here as the banker who was, sadly, "the last of the breed." Whenever a gathering of Vermont business owners gathers, it's only a matter of time until they begin to tell Dudley Davis stories.

For years, Dudley Davis was THE decision-maker at Merchants Bank. Merchants, founded in 1849, remains Vermont's only independent, statewide community bank. But what made Dudley unique is that, unlike most bankers, he didn't base his funding decision solely on the numbers. Instead, he followed his gut instincts and bet on people. Stories abound of business owners approaching Dudley with a fact-filled, fifty-page business plan, only to see him put it aside and never even glance through it. Dudley's decisions, apparently, were based on the look in your eye and the strength of your handshake.

Moreover, if you ran into trouble down the road, as most growing businesses do, Dudley would not leave you hanging. Many Vermont businesses owe their existence to their financial partnership with Merchants Bank.

There were other Dudley Davises running community banks in towns throughout the U.S. at that time. Like George Bailey in the movie It's a Wonderful Life, the local banker was once an integral part of the community fabric. As the financial world has consolidated and centralized, however, you don't hear as many good Dudley Davis stories any more. Gut instincts, level gazes, and firm handshakes don't count for as much in the modern financial world.

Of course, Dudley was no one's fool when it came to finance. He often received a point or two premium for taking a greater risk. The student center at the University of Vermont stands as testament that his judgments were fundamentally sound.

So, as you get off I-89 at Exit 14 and head toward downtown Burlington on Williston Road, passing through the UVM campus overlooking Lake Champlain, on your right you will pass the gleaming Dudley Davis Student Center. "Dudley Davis," you might logically conclude, is a guy who did some things very well. And you would be right. Entrepreneurs worldwide mourn the passing of an era.

Chapter 13
The Pyramid Scheme

I solve the Key Bank problem by finding a venture capitalist to take out their debt. Now I've got a venture capital problem.

Martin Kelly and I develop an ambitious plan to take Magic Hat national and to become a dominant company in the craft brewing world. We find a willing partner in a successful hedge fund. We set the plan in motion by acquiring Pyramid Breweries in Seattle, only to have the rules change abruptly when the economy crashes in 2008.

Lesson: Trading Monkeys

I finally got the Key Bank monkey off my back when I found a venture capitalist to buy out our debt. Venture capital (VC) is money invested in early-stage start-ups with the prospect of a high rate of return through an eventual realization event, such as the sale of a company or a stock offering. As such, a brewing business, which is capital-intensive and a commodity business, is not as good a prospect for VC as a technology company.

My experience is that people in the VC firms are, as a group, smart, rich, risk takers, and snakes, notorious for being charming during the courtship period and deadly as soon as things don't work out as planned. Perhaps there are exceptions, but my experience has been that this community really only values one thing, return on their investment.

My new financial partner was Todd Enright, who definitely fit the snake mode, but I thought of him as MY snake, fearsome and ferocious to the outside world, but a friendly pet to us.

Todd was especially good at finding value in distressed properties, and Magic Hat was a distressed property. Luckily, we were his one soft spot. He was our financial partner for the next nine years. It was a relationship that was occasionally uneasy but one that saw us mature greatly as a business and grow into a regional powerhouse.

I met Todd initially when he dropped in, unannounced, at our Flynn Ave. brewery. He was young—he looked like he was right out of college— smart, and arrogant, with plenty of attitude. He announced "I'm a venture capitalist, and I'd like to invest in Magic Hat."

Thank you very much, I replied, but we're not interested at this time. I'd hear back from him periodically, just reminding us that he was out there. I didn't really give him a second thought until we got the letter from Key Bank telling us to come up with more than a million bucks in ten days. Hello, Todd?

While Todd was very flexible in how he made money, he specialized in distressed properties, mostly real estate. He'd buy a property, or bundle of properties, sell off enough to recoup his investment, then the rest would be gravy. Usually, he'd be into and out of a deal within twelve months.

A good example of how he worked came when a brewery in Key West, Florida came on the market. Once again, we did not have the cash needed to increase capacity, and they had some holding tanks that we coveted. But the property was being sold lock, stock, and barrel, real estate and all. We couldn't deal with the whole package, but Todd stepped in and bought it, then sold us all the equipment for a reasonable price (and financed it for us), allowing us to sell off any of the equipment we did not need in order to keep the tanks we needed at no cost to us. He made a nice profit, but we got the tanks without being encumbered by all the other pieces.

For the next nine years, Todd was, in effect, our chief financial officer. He wasn't the most reliable guy, and he didn't always deliver what he said he'd deliver when he said he'd deliver it, but there's no denying his financial brilliance. He was a master of the balance sheet, and there were two or three times when he pulled our asses out of the fire, either by investing in us when no one else would or by pointing us toward solutions to complex problems.

Sometimes Todd would go too far. One time when we needed money, he bargained for a piece of the pie (that is, shares of the company) that I thought was excessive. But we had no choice. When we finally settled, I held out a set of keys.

"What are these?" he asked.

"The keys to the front door," I replied, "because you've now removed any incentive for me to stay." Todd got the point and renegotiated the deal to a more equitable level.

There's not a doubt in my mind that Magic Hat would have gone belly-up long before it did without the services of Todd Enright. What I particularly appreciated is that he didn't jam his solutions down our throats, but rather led me to make the conclusions that he thought were right. I learned a lot from Todd.

Although Key Bank was no longer in the picture, our financial problems were far from solved. In reality, what we did was replace one monkey on our back with another. We had some breathing room now, but it came with crushing debt that continued to eat up most of our operating capital. Sorry, Stacey, but you'll just have to make that box of T-shirts last.

The business eventually got too big for Bob, just as Seventh Generation had when I had originally hired him to work in the warehouse. This is a guy who is more an artist than a businessperson, and now he found himself managing three shifts of fifty people, and trying to write a three-year projection for our grain needs. As time went on, it became obvious that we needed a professional manufacturing type running that part of the business, not a craftsperson on steroids.

Pushing Bob out the door was not easy for either of us. As much as anyone, he was the heart and soul of the Magic Hat brewery, but he wasn't the right person for the job anymore. He and I were both relieved when we negotiated a settlement, and I'm proud to count Bob as one of my closest business associates of all time—and still a personal friend..

Today, Bob is back in Portland, Maine, operating a bakery. Here's what he said in an article about me in Vermont Business Magazine in 2006: "I grow businesses, get to a certain level, but I like the more small and intimate side of things. And I love start-ups. . . . It was a very fair and generous settlement agreement. Very fair, very generous. I love Alan dearly. He is absolutely one of my closest friends. . . . He's also one of the most difficult people I've ever worked with. He's also one of the smartest people. . . . He pushes you. He pushed me into trying things like beer styles." He also said that my greatest strength was my ability to create chaos, and "when you're growing a business as fast as we did it, you want comfort. But you need to create chaos. You have to think outside the box."

The person we brought in to take us to the next stage of development was Martin Kelly. A year later, in 2004, it was my time to step aside. Luckily for me, rather than being pushed out the door, I was pushed up the ladder. Martin had just been relieved of his duties as CEO of the Pyramid Breweries in Seattle. Originally, we hired him to write a five-year plan for Magic Hat. When this three-month task was completed, I sensed that he was excited about the plan and our prospects for growth, so I asked him, "Given all the work you put into this plan, do you really want to leave it to me to execute? Why not commute across the country, at half your regular salary, to make it work?" And he said yes.

Martin is a self-described "corporate gypsy" who has worked for Coca-Cola, Miller Brewing Company, and Borden Foods. He also knew the craft brewing world from his time at Pyramid. We hired him as Potentate, Pilot & Primary Prestidigitator (P4), while I became chairman and chief creative officer.

I had known Martin for a few years at this point. We had served on the board of the craft beer trade association of that time (the Brewers Association of America) and frequently found ourselves being the only two people in the room that would agree on issues. I was always impressed with how smart Martin was (maybe because he agreed with me), and I had visited him in California a few times when he ran Pyramid and frequently called him for suggestions on how to deal with situations we were facing. Martin was the real deal when it came to managing a sales-and-distribution business.

In manufacturing terms, we were now entering the big leagues, and I knew I was no longer the right person to be in charge of operations. By this time, Magic Hat was the tenth-largest craft brewer in the country.

Martin's task, in his own words, was to "build the relevance of our existing brands in existing markets and grow market share; continuously evolve our portfolio of beers to keep it fresh, interesting and relevant to our community of consumers; and maintain our methodical expansion into new markets." Martin described my job like this: "As chairman, he participates in the development of the strategic plans for the company, approving the operating and capital budgets as well as any external financing issues. As chief creative, he is intimately involved in the evolution of the look and feel of the brand, and also contributes to the development of the marketing plan. From a new business development standpoint, he prospects for new territories for us to enter, evaluates new product ideas, and otherwise think of new ways for us to expand the reach and strength of the brand."

Magic Hat now employed seventy-five people and had a distribution area that stretched from Maine to North Carolina and as far west as Pittsburgh. I watched in glee as the company entered a period of explosive growth. We dropped some products; added new ones; expanded the distribution area; put the brand in chain supermarkets, chain convenience stores and chain restaurants; and increased sales from $9 million in 2004 to $11.5 million in 2005.

The part of the business plan that had both Martin and me so excited was something called a roll-up. This is a strategy used by investors (usually private-equity firms) where multiple small companies in the same market are acquired and merged, reducing costs through economies of scale. Roll-ups also have the effect of increasing the valuation multiples a business can command as it acquires increased market share. Roll-ups also weaken competition in crowded and fragmented markets, where there are many small, struggling players but room for only a few to succeed.

And this was exactly the terrain in the brewing industry in 2004. The growth of the craft beer business had attracted hundreds of yahoos like Bob and Alan. From a low of forty-two independent brewers in 1978, the ranks had swelled to more than a thousand, many of them, like Magic Hat, strong regionally but only marginally profitable.

Remember Bucky Fuller's notion about bigger and smaller? After Prohibition ended, there were 750 operating breweries. By 1978, there were only 42 left, the colorful regional firms having given way to the Buds, Millers, and Coors of the world. During the 1990s, most of the craft brewers in America experienced strong growth, which was fueled by the growth of the overall category of specialty beers. By 2004, however, Martin and I both felt that the national thirst for craft product would inevitably flatten, especially now that the category was substantial enough to attract the attention of the big boys.

One of the ongoing conversations Martin and I had over

the years was that as the category of craft beers grew, it would attract the attention of the larger American breweries as well as the large imported beer companies. Our concern was that if we did not somehow build some mass and accumulate some cash, we would never be able to compete because the big boys would control the distributors and therefore the availability of our beer.

How times have changed—do you think your father ever imagined he would see a beer like Bud Light Lime in the grocer's cooler? Or a Budweiser wheat beer? Or Coors making a "Belgium-style white beer?

Our idea was to put together a group of independent craft breweries with different geographic and brand strengths, with a national sales-and-distribution system, and try to build enough scale with these combined smaller brands to be able to compete with the larger (non-craft) companies entering the field.

We saw consolidation on the horizon, and the opportunities this would present—if we were prepared to manage them. We would also have to be able to afford them, as acquisitions require substantial capital. Between my ability to build brands and Martin's management experience, we thought we had the complete package. All we needed was more money.

To make a roll-up work, we needed deeper pockets than Todd's. The money that would be required to execute this strategy was more than Todd could afford or was willing to risk.

Things had begun to change between Magic Hat and Todd. His lifestyle changed dramatically from spartan to extravagant. He bought two airplanes—a twin-engine turboprop and a small jet. He built a new house in the horse country of southern Georgia. He took up fox hunting and other pursuits of the über-rich. He seemed to be working less, and I got the impression that fewer and fewer of his deals were succeeding. Once, we had a deal for a bank loan to finance further expansion, but it collapsed due to Todd's failure to deliver some needed financials, almost as if he didn't want the loan to happen. Something was wrong.

Brimming with confidence and empowered by a "can't miss" strategy, Martin and I set off to find a brewery to buy. Meanwhile, Magic Hat had worked out the kinks from its rocky transition from glorified home brewery to real business. We were now present in all major markets in the Northeast, including a very successful entry into the notoriously tough New York City market.

And we found a brewery to buy, which—surprise of surprises—was Martin's former employer, Pyramid! No one believes this, but buying Pyramid was not even on the radar screen when we brought Martin on board. It just turned out they were available and fit our criteria.

Despite the developing uneasiness of our relation with Todd, the Pyramid deal moved forward. We had known that the roll-up would require deeper pockets than Todd's, so earlier we had added an additional financial partner at a very low level of ownership, Basso Capital Management, L.P. (BCM), a hedge fund based in Stamford, Connecticut. The firm had been founded in 2003 and is employee-owned, providing services to pooled investment vehicles. A hedge fund is a private investment fund that invests in diverse assets and employs a variety of investment strategies to maintain a hedged portfolio intended to protect the fund's investors from downturns in the market and to maximize returns on market upswings.

Translated: they play a high-risk, high-stakes business gambling game. Here's the other salient factor: in 2007 many hedge funds, including Basso, were rolling in dough. In four short years I heard they had accumulated more than $2 billion under their management. Their biggest issue, as it was explained to me, was where to invest all the money that new investors were throwing at them.

Magic Hat was a good candidate for a hedge fund. We were profitable. We had huge upside potential. We were a regional powerhouse, with a healthy brand and potential to go national. We had solid, professional management in place. Not only did

Martin have experience with larger companies, but he also had intimate knowledge about his former employer, Pyramid Breweries.

The deal we worked out was fairly straightforward. As I remember it, Todd would own something like 40 percent of Magic Hat, Basso 40 percent, and I would retain 20 percent with some of my original investors. I liked the deal, because in order for any major decision to be made, two of the three owners would have to agree, and despite our misgivings, Todd and I now had a nine-year track record of making decisions that were in the best interests of Magic Hat. But I also understood that I was in a very high-stakes game, and those coals under my feet were getting warm.

Life: Mom Is Right Again

Remember my mom's theory of "More So"? It was to be proven again. I had observed Todd's modus operandi in dealing with other companies, but somehow I thought things would be different in his dealings with Magic Hat. He could be ruthless with other people, but I thought he was my friend and that the rules were different for me—just as I had previously thought in regard to my previous business/ financial partner, Jeff Hollander.

I was about to find out differently. Our lawyer got a call from a beer distributor, one that we weren't particularly fond of, asking for financial details about Magic Hat that we considered to be completely confidential. Our response, translated, was "Who the *&@!! do you think you are? That kind of information is available only to the owners of the company."

"But," came the response, "we are an owner of the company."

It was clearly within Todd's right to do what he did, but it was also a clear violation of my personal trust that he did it without telling me. Although we had been through the brewing wars together, now our interests were far apart. Very quickly and very quietly it was arranged for Basso to buy out Todd's interest in Magic Hat. Another movie had ended, and the next one was about to begin. The new movie cast me in more of a supporting role as a minority partner with limited say and rights.

Chapter 14
Exit Strategies

*I get a crash course in realities. We move forward with
our plan to buy Pyramid. Instantly, Magic Hat is on top
of the craft brewing world. Just as instantly we find out
that straddling two coasts and two company cultures is
a huge challenge.*

*Then the world implodes: the U.S. economy tanks
in September 2008, and hedge funds, which were the
highest fliers, are among the fastest to plummet. The
cool little brewery roll-up scheme that made sense
only a couple of years earlier now seems like a lapse in
financial sanity. Martin and I scramble like crazy to get
it all to work, but the bullet fired by Key Bank back in
1997 finally claims its victim.*

If only I had remembered Judy's sage advice not to get on the
road unless you want to go where the road goes. Now I was
involved in a game that had little to do with beer or brand, but
a lot to do with money. If only I hadn't demanded that Miller
post a $5 million bond. If only I hadn't taken the loan from
Key Bank. If only I could be back on a porch overlooking Lake
Champlain sipping homebrews with Bob. Just keep walking,
Alan. There's no turning back.

Basso Capital Management bought out Todd's loan
participation and took his financial piece of the Pyramid deal.
On the surface nothing changed, but in reality, the balance of
power had tipped overwhelmingly in their favor. They were

now the majority owner and could do (just about) anything they wanted, whether I liked it or not. I signed the drag-along clause that would eventually come back to bite me. I asked for and received an employment contract that would allow me to leave the company with that employment contract intact, should they ever sell their share in a deal I did not approve. I was now more employee than owner. I fully understood the risk at the time, but at least with this new contract in hand, I could not be "sold" to a new acquirer without my consent.

Over the years, I had watched many of my friends lose their companies to "the money people" and had only once seen the entrepreneur remain with the new company and achieve any level of success after the changeover. That one, Hinda Miller, sold her company, Jogbra (which she had co-founded with Lisa Lindall), to Playtex. I always marveled at Hinda for making this transition but swore I would never even attempt it.

Here are Hinda's thoughts on why and how she made that transition:

Hinda Miller on Transition to the Corporate World

My partner and I were ready to sell. We were exhausted. We needed new capital, new computers, new talent, and new markets. As 50/50 owners, we always had a very rocky relationship. After twelve years, we were burnt out and neither of us wanted to deal with more personalities and demands. So, when we got "The Call" with an offer to buy the company, we both looked at the offer very seriously. At the time, we felt we got a fair price from Playtex, which was then sold to Sara Lee Corp. within the year.

My partner decided to leave. I decided to stay. I was curious about corporate life. Knowing my personality and work history, I could have never risen up the corporate ladder. When I was given an opportunity to lead my division, I took it. I stayed for six years as president of the Champion Jogbra division of Sara Lee Corporation.

I loved Jogbra and wanted to lead the transition for the sake of the employees, vendors, and customers. At the company, we had a saying, "Change is good." I truly believed that change is the only reality. My father had always encouraged me to do the things that frightened me. So moving through fear was familiar to me. At that point in my spiritual evolution, I knew a little about the inner workings of the ego and the benefits of non-attachment. Besides, I was always attracted to the Buddhist concept of the "beginner's mind," always living in the world as a student. I also never adopted the stresses of having to be perfect, so making mistakes was just part of the learning process.

Looking back now, I feel like I earned an M.B.A. at Sara Lee Corporation. I saw corporate life as another challenge with new personalities, priorities, and politics.

Hinda Miller, Co-Founder, Jogra Inc.
Vermont State Senator

Life Continues:

Back to my story: With all these new agreements now in place, the Pyramid deal moved forward and we eventually acquired them for $25.2 million. If we could pull off the roll-up strategy successfully, then this movie could still have a happy ending. Now might have been a good moment in the history of Magic Hat to hit the "pause" button and for us to ask ourselves, "Do we want to keep on keeping on as a solid regional company, or do we want to go for the brass ring of becoming a national company?" People still ask me (as they do about Key Bank) if

I would make the same decision, and my response is the same: "DO I LOOK LIKE AN IDIOT?"

That said, given the same circumstances and information that existed at the time, I would do the same thing a hundred times out of a hundred. Don't worry about those glowing coals, I'd tell Martin. They won't burn your feet. Hop in, Martin, we're going for a little plane ride. I'm sure we'll find some place to land.

Pyramid Breweries was among the early micros, having opened in Seattle in 1984. I had been a fan for years. They offered a broad variety of craft beers, ales, and lagers under the Pyramid label, and under another label, MacTarnahan's. It also has brewpubs in Sacramento, Berkeley, and Walnut Creek, California, and a very successful restaurant in Seattle, right across the street from the stadium where the Seattle Mariners played. Among the products bottled under the Pyramid brand are Amber Weizen (a dark wheat ale), Apricot Weizen (a fruit beer), Thunderhead IPA, Curve Ball Kölsch, and Snow Cap (a winter warmer).

The company was founded in Kalama, Washington in 1984 as Hart Brewing, Inc.; in 1992, they bought Thomas Kemper Brewing, a company in Poulsbo, Washington; and in 1996 they finally changed their name to Pyramid.

The company went public, but became private again when we acquired it in August 2008 for $2.75 per share. Included in the deal were their four restaurants (called "Alehouses") in Seattle, Berkeley, Walnut Creek, and Sacramento and a taproom in Portland, Oregon.

Let's see . . . what else happened in 2008? Barack Obama was elected president in November, and . . . oh yeah, the economy crashed and burned in September. Hedge funds, being the highest rollers, were hit the heaviest, and Basso Capital Management was no exception. Their assets shrunk to a fraction of what they had been earlier in the year. A little brewery in Vermont, seemingly a good prospect for a national roll-up only a few months before, was suddenly a distraction.

Martin and I knew we were toast at this point, but we soldiered on, hoping to find that gas station in the sky (Arnie Koss's airplane analogy again; see Chapter 2). Maybe Magic Hat could be acquired by a classy European brewery, one that wanted a foothold in the American craft beer market and who appreciated the brand we had established with Magic Hat. Maybe the economy would rebound and we could move forward with the original strategy. It was not a situation without hope; however, it was a situation best described as "tenuous."

Basso needed to sell their participation in what was now called Independent Brewers United (IBU), the rolled-up company, i.e., the parent company we created in 2008 when we bought Pyramid. Our daily connection with Basso was Greg Gatta. I knew we were not in a strong negotiating position, but I did make one request, as I mentioned in Chapter 2: if IBU was to be sold, please don't sell it to KPS Capital Partners, L.P., a private equity fund, which was doing their own brewery roll-up plan. (That plan would create KPS's new portfolio company, North American Breweries in 2009.) By 2010 they had already acquired four breweries, including Genesee, and were, in my opinion, not the best possible fit."

It didn't help our situation that our acquisition of Pyramid had not been going smoothly. To be blunt, it was a disaster. There were two fundamental issues: Money was one: as soon as the deal was done, all our financing fell apart with the banking crisis. Suddenly we did not have the capital we thought we would need to make this work unless everything worked perfectly. And it did not. We learned a lot. The second big issue was a clash of cultures: entrepreneurial versus corporate. The culture of Magic Hat was entrepreneurial, a spirit that rippled through every part of the company from our field sales force to the accounting department; whereas Pyramid, as a publically held company, had a more corporate mentality. While I saw Magic Hat employees as being energetic and solution-oriented, the people at Pyramid were governed by attitudes that put compliance above all else.

The original idea was that Martin would manage the parent company (IBU), and I would be the IBU marketing director with specific responsibility for the Magic Hat brand. In reality, though, for a bunch of reasons, I had little to do with the Pyramid or MacTarnahan's brands and was never happy with how this was handled.

Looking back, I learned two things. I should have been much more involved with the other brands. Entrepreneurs are not generally known for their patience, but this is one instance where I was too slow to pull the trigger. And I should have made staff changes earlier, because if the culture doesn't work, nothing else will. One positive thing I will say about how North American Breweries executed the KPS acquisition of IBU, they were clear: you will be on our plan, or get out. I would embrace this approach next time I'm running a company and acquire another company—if there is a "next time."

Morever, we spent eighteen months operating in a void of financial data. We would have straightened things out eventually, but once the bottom fell out of the economy, we knew it would be very difficult to survive. Those final months, when we were totally out of money and waiting for the other shoe to drop, were some of the hardest, most unpleasant, and frustrating of my professional career.

Our relationship with Greg Gatta was deteriorating. Clearly, he was there to represent Basso's interests, not ours. Our fear was that he was becoming far more concerned about his own future than ours or the fate of our brands. Basso's gamble on our roll-up in 2008 had not paid off, and the timing could not have been worse. I knew the days of Magic Hat as an independent entity—and me as its spiritual leader—were numbered. I no longer had a platform with any power, but repeated my one request: that the company not be sold to KPS and added into the North American Breweries roll-up with other, totally different brands including Labatt Blue and Dundee Brewing.

In June 2010, while I was on a motorcycle trip to Maine with the boys, I got "The E-mail" (the cyber-version of "The Call") from Gatta, summoning Martin and me back to Burlington the next night to have dinner with the new owners. Although he neglected to mention who that new owner was, I knew immediately. The sale to North American Breweries was finalized in August,. The bullet that had been fired back in 1997 finally claimed its victim.

Carpe diem,
quam minimum
credule postero.

– Horace, Odes *circa 23 BCE*

Seize the day,
trust tomorrow minimally.

Chapter 15
Carpe Diem

Entrepreneurs look forward, not back, and as the bloated bulge of baby boomers look forward, what they see is . . . opportunity. In this thrilling and insightful conclusion, I bring together all of life's lessons to reveal the meaning of life (and assorted short subjects).

Because of the businesses I have been involved with, somewhere along the line I get at least some credit for being among the founding fathers of "businesses for social responsibility." Whether it is deserved or not is debatable, and whether it is meaningful or not is even more debatable.

Life: The Game Show

Now we enter the lightning round, where all answers count double and our winning contestant will be invited back to defend his/her crown next week. I figure I will never write another book, so here are a few unsolicited opinions that I want to include:

◆ *Businesses for Social Responsibility*
The idea for an actual association of like-minded businesses in Vermont grew out of informal meetings that Matt Rubin (then developing a hydro project in Winooski), Dave Barasch (then the human resources guy at Ben & Jerry's), and I held. None of us ever imagined this would eventually grow into the state's

second-largest trade association for businesses, behind only the Chamber of Commerce.

A lot of other names are mentioned when the subject of socially responsible business comes up. Several of them—Lyman Wood, Ben Cohen, Will Raap, Jeffrey Hollender—are characters in this book. Even though my name is occasionally mentioned with theirs, it's not a credit I really deserve or seek.

I think Lyman Wood's practice of paying people double for vacations is one of the most enlightened, humane, and socially responsible ideas ever, but guess what? I've never had it as a policy in any of the businesses I've owned or operated. I could never afford it. Start-up businesses are stimulating, invigorating, exciting, and even inspiring, but they are not pretty. Remember Bob Johnson's description of people bumping into each other and smashing their knuckles in the refrigeration room and Matty's story about entering the fermentation room at the Flynn Avenue brewery? That's a start-up. In a good one, you are guaranteed to find great people who are all overworked and underpaid.

I get a chuckle when I go to one of these socially responsible business gatherings and have the vice-president of some bank telling me how "s.r." he is because, for any employee who buys a bike to ride to work, he pays half the cost of the bike. Equally amusing is the would-be entrepreneur who wants to talk about triple bottom lines before he has a double or single.

Social responsibility is not a slogan, not a marketing strategy, but a way of life. It is not about counting paper clips, nor is it about self-aggrandizing mission statements. It's about where your vendors get their resources, what chemicals are used in processing those resources, how the by-products are disposed of, how they treat their work force. The hard work includes knowing how your own product affects the waste stream, and owning up to customers when products don't perform as promised. To me, being socially responsible as a business is akin to being a good neighbor to your community.

◆ Firewalking

For a few years in the 1980s, my enthusiasm for firewalking was so great that whenever Tony Robbins brought his traveling road show to Vermont, I volunteered to prepare the fires for the climactic firewalk. When the fire was fully prepared, the first guy to march across was usually me.

Eventually I learned the truth about firewalking. It's not a trick and Tony Robbins is not a magician, but its lessons are just as valid. There's a reason why this has been used as a test of an individual's strength and courage in ceremonies for thousands of years. Glowing coals are not great conductors of heat. While the heat, collectively, from a group of coals is intense enough to char-broil a steak (or your feet), the coals themselves are ineffective conductors of the heat, so that brief contact with them will not result in a burn. If you can conquer your fear, make that first step and keep walking, you'll be ok.

But don't try this at home, kiddies.

◆ Organized religion

I'm a spiritual person, but I'm not a big fan of organized religion. More destruction and carnage has been done in the name of religion than anything else.

◆ Socially Responsible Investing

The Socially Responsible Investment sector has grown to be a trillion-dollar industry. Many of these types of funds produce handsome brochures that liberally use terms like "microloan," "third world," and "AIDS awareness."

None of the companies or funds that call themselves "socially responsible" ever invested a nickel in any of the businesses I was involved with. However green the mantle rest assured that the decisions are made by the money guys, not by social activists.

◆ Fair Trade

This is one of the rare cases where a business practice has made a meaningful difference in the world, at least for coffee growers. I may not be giving the right technical definition of "fair trade" here, but my understanding is that it is a business practice in which the buying partnership between farmer and buyer is determined by what the farmer needs to live on rather than what the market will bear. The higher initial cost, all other things being equal, is eventually reflected in a higher price at the consumer level. If the consumer values sustainable commerce enough to pay the price, then it's win-win-win-win for farmer, trader, retailer, and consumer.

The same principle has been applied on a limited basis in the dairy industry, notably by the Organic Valley Co-op members. Maybe if we could get Fair Trade practices applied to conventional dairies, we could save Vermont family farms from going under. (Heard the one about the dairy farmer who won the lottery? Asked what he will be doing with the windfall, he replies "Just keep farming 'til it's all gone.)

Because of the willingness of even mainstream companies such as Starbucks, Ben & Jerry's, and Green Mountain Coffee Roasters to commit to Fair Trade coffee, a lot of marginal coffee farmers in Central America are still on their land. And we can get wonderful shade-grown, organic coffee even at McDonald's these days.

◆ The Magic of the Vermont Brand

It's heresy to say this, but I don't think including the name "Vermont" does anything to enhance most brands. The people in Vermont's office of business development will be furious with me for popping this balloon, but I believe that there is no more magic to "Vermont" in brand building than "Delaware" or "South Dakota." Sorry.

But what about Vermont Teddy Bear?

What about Green Mountain Coffee Roasters?

These are companies that have been successful because they are well-run businesses that have done a superb job of executing their business plans. They have succeeded in spite of, rather than because of, their branding.

Occasionally there is a logical association between the name "Vermont" and a product or service. One of the clearest associations people have with the state is the &^%$*!! cold weather here. Therefore, if you are offering a product that keeps you warm in winter, Vermont is a logical association. Would you be more likely to buy a woodstove from the Vermont Stove Company or the Jamaican Stove Company?

But coffee? Mmm-m-m just give me a cup of that local java, grown on the shaded hillsides of Camel's Hump Mountain.

There is also a Vermont Coffee Company founded by Paul Ralston, another veteran from the local entrepreneurial battlefield. Like Green Mountain Coffee Roasters, Paul's company is also very successful, but on an entirely different scale. Whereas GMCR is a behemoth with a market-cap value in the billions of dollars, Vermont Coffee is an intentionally small scale operation with a handful of employees and a limited distribution area—limited enough that Paul has enough time to serve in the Vermont House of Representatives. He probably wouldn't have that luxury if he were an executive at GMCR.

My point is that these two companies are successful because of their smart execution of their business strategies, not because of the magic of their names. If you don't believe that, then I think Ethan Allen Coffee Company and Catamount Beans are still available names.

Ironically, two of the companies most often cited for their branding brilliance are Ben & Jerry's and Cabot Cheese. Let's see—Ben & Jerry's are two Jewish guys from Long Island who featured photos of themselves swathed in tie-dye and with long, untamed hair on their product packaging. What marketing

morons! Wouldn't they have done much better if they had
called it the Vermont Ice Cream Company? And instead of
those goofy flavor names, they could have come up with
Vermont-associated names such as Middle Berry and Calvin
Coolidge Crunch.

I'm not saying that Vermont was not a key part of the
overall brand identity, but that it was only that—a part of it.

◆ Doctors

I've already covered this subject.

◆ Employees

I get very irritated when I hear people complaining about their
employees. The offending line is usually "You just can't get good
help these days." It's demeaning, as if they are lamenting the
lack of good pastrami in the world.

My experience is that most people want to succeed. Think
about it. Does anyone ever get out of bed in the morning and
say, "I think I will fail today! It's a great day for failure." If you're
a business owner, it's YOUR job to create an environment
where it's possible for everyone to succeed. If you are
reasonably diligent about who you hire and you create the right
environment for success, not only will your employees succeed,
but they will make you successful, too. This is doubly true for
any employees who are on any kind of variable compensation
where their income is dependent on commissions or bonuses.
You want your employees to make their commissions! You want
them to earn their bonuses! They are making you successful in
the process.

And yet, I don't know how many times I've heard owners
complain that their top sales person is making more money
than they do. (OK, I will permit a brief, sympathetic whine.)
Again, this is what you should want. Reverse the situation.
What if you were saying "My top sales person is barely making

a livable wage. Next quarter I think I can get her down below the poverty level."

It just doesn't make sense. I have continually been impressed, and honored, at the great lengths the employees of my companies will go to make me look good and to increase the value of my business. People aren't broken, but some business environments are very broken.

◆ *Beer Geeks*

This next statement won't win me any friends in the beer world, but one of the industry problems these days are the beer geeks. They are a very small but highly vocal and influential segment. Unfortunately, from a brewer's perspective, they are fickle and elusive and have pushed beer into "wine-ification." They are on an eternal quest for beers that are ever-stronger, ever-hoppier, and ever more novel. Thus, their quest leads them to the small and obscure breweries that can satisfy the unquenchable thirst for the undiscovered. This, in turn, helps create the exact world they are trying to avoid—one controlled by the big brewers.

For some reason, they don't seem to understand that breweries are businesses, and businesses need capital for things such as capacity, quality control, and sales and marketing activities, including distributor sales incentives. This is where the large domestic and large import breweries have the advantage—and they use their cash advantage to improve their distribution. Without distribution, you cannot sell your beer.

The new rage is the "craft beer bar" with 100+ different beers being offered. No draft beer will be kept longer than two to four weeks (and draft beer, in the business, is known to be where you get sampling of your product). This makes it very hard for any craft beer brand to build a following.

The large craft brewers like Sam Adams, Magic Hat, New Belgium, and Sierra Nevada are the craft breweries that are investing in their businesses to improve quality, to sell to those learning to drink craft beer, which in turn grows the market share of the entire category. The geeks are like the wine snobs eternally on the quest for that limited-production zinfandel that's made by the one-armed vintner who makes six bottles a year. I love the unusual as much as the next guy, but these beers will not grow the category of craft beers, but, rather, will compete based on the novelty factor. But today, more and more beer is being sold as the wine industry does now: by style and price, not by brand. If we don't financially support the brands, they cannot develop the cash flow to compete against the larger domestic and import companies who will eventually win if the game is reduced to style and PRICE.

Let's take solace in the fact that United States, once the barren wasteland of the beer world, is now the richest beer terrain on the planet. And the transition has occurred in little more than two decades.

There—I'm all done. Thanks for letting me vent!

Life, Times, and Lessons:

Here's the grand finale.

Creating a viable business is not easy, and it's certainly not for the faint of heart. Too often our heroes turn out to have feet of clay, and that proved the case with Marshall Thurber, my father, Jeffrey Hollander, and Todd Enright. The closer I came to these people, the less I liked what I saw, but that is not to deny their skills and talents and the seminal roles they played in my own business career. Others—Lyman, Will, Ben, and my mother come to mind—have held up well or even gained in stature over time.

I came from a world of abundance. My father operated with total disregard to where the next dollar was coming from. His assumption was that it would always be there. As I look back, I can see in myself that same independent streak he had—and that same sense that I'll always be able to find a way to make money, I'll always be able to cover the mortgage, I'll always be able to put food on the table.

My greatest teacher has been failure. And I have absolutely no fear of failing again. Maybe that's the definition of being an entrepreneur.

I don't have regrets. Even when I was at KaramelKorn, which was the worst period of my life, I learned to never do something solely for the money (because if the money is not there, you have bupkis). From the yacht time-share idea, I learned that too much money can kill a business just as easily as not enough money. I also learned not to smuggle pot into the U.S. on an airplane. At Gardens for All/Gardener's Supply Company I learned the difference between a for-profit and a non-profit, but, more important, I learned that my personal values could be brought into a business environment.

From Seventh Generation, oh my God!, I learned to be a little more financially cautious, to build a stronger base, and never to believe my press clippings; and that I'm never as smart as I look when things are going well, and when things are hitting the wall and dying around me, I'm not that stupid, either.

Here's a story about death . . . and bankers. It demonstrates that quirky sense of humor I seem to have, which Ross referred to (in Chapter 12).

In 1998, Magic Hat was in "workout mode" with our bank. This is what happens when borrowers find themselves in over their heads. To avoid foreclosure or default, the borrower and lender create a workout program in which they agree to certain benchmarks and goals. With my well-documented attitudes toward authority, you can imagine how much I liked operating under these restrictions. When you don't have any other options, however . . .

The bank representative who was put in charge of our plan—well, let's just refer to him as Pip Squeak. Without wanting to prejudice your perception of him, I would describe him as young, rude, arrogant, and a completely detestable person. Moreover, his attitude could be summarized as "If you're so smart, how come you're the one in workout, and I'm the one in charge?"

G-r-r-r.

Young Pippy and I had a meeting scheduled for the following Friday. It was an important meeting where I was to present my "plan for working out" of the financial mess we were in at the time, and he warned me to be prepared. No problem. I had a business trip the previous week that took me to southern New England. Since I was in the area, I thought I'd pop into New York City over the weekend and visit my mother. When she didn't answer the door, I entered her apartment and found her unconscious in a coma on the floor.

I called 9-1-1, and the ambulance came and took here to

the hospital, where they confirmed the worst—that there was no chance she would come out of it. My mother had prepared well for death, and prepared me well for this moment. Under no circumstances did she want to be kept alive artificially. She had taken care of all the necessary paperwork, the living will, etc. Moreover, she had drilled me on what to do if I found her in exactly this situation.

The medical establishment has its own built-in checks and balances to insure that no one acts prematurely, so it was several days before we could make the decision to end her life. Even though she had thoroughly prepared me for it, it wasn't an easy thing to do, and afterward there seemed like an overwhelming number of details and arrangements to take care of.

One of these was to call Pippy to say that we'd have to postpone our Friday meeting.

"Alan," he sternly interrupted me when I started to explain, "there is no reason on earth you can think of to postpone this meeting." So instead of telling him what happened, I baited him first with clichés such as "Sometimes life's challenges overwhelm what we might have committed to," to which he kept responding, "There can be no excuses," until I finally said, "Sorry, but my mother just died." It was the only time I heard Pip Squeak go silent. Thank you, Mom!

. . . which brings me to hippies.

Some people think that hippies are just countercultural types from the 1960s who made style statements with their clothes and hair. When the sociologists of 2050 look back, however, I think they will give hippies their due as the movers and shakers of the modern era.

There was World War II—which we won, by the way— followed by the "Great Sleep" that was the 1950s, when the nation focused on the goal of quantity and forgot how to do anything and everything with the goal of quality. We forgot how to grow our own food; we forgot how to make real bread; we forgot how to brew real beer. Women even forgot how to have babies—they went into hospitals pregnant and woke up with babies. And no breast feeding, when "formula" is so much better.

People like my mother were victims of the '50s. They forgot how to live (at least for a while).

The children of the '50s, including me, grew up angry at their idyllic world. Is life really like the TV show "Leave It to Beaver?" My mother wasn't June. My father wasn't Ward. My brother wasn't Wally. (Actually, as the older brother, I wasn't Wally, and my little brother wasn't da Beav.) My friends, however, were all Lumpys and Eddie Haskells.

Then came the '60s. We Baby Boomers were ready to take things back. Look at the world we were given: immaculate suburbs and decaying downtowns, Wonder Bread and Budweiser, Velveeta and Cheese Whiz in an aerosol can, shopping malls and KaramelKorn, the L.A. Dodgers and San Francisco Giants. We were ready to take things back.

The assassinations and Vietnam were the excuses. The Beatles, Woodstock, and The Haight were the symbols, but it was going to happen anyway. We were going to take control. We claimed our personal freedoms with books and magazines such as Our Bodies, Ourselves and the Mother Earth News—popular tomes of our times, teaching women to care for their own health needs and all of us how to live independently. We demanded legal rights with laws such as Roe v. Wade and the Miranda Act.

But we were not ready to take control when we were twenty—nor when we were thirty (this would take the forefront of the Baby Boomers to 1976) and too busy with kids and careers to make waves. But then we hit forty, and we were ready to rock 'n' roll.

And that's pretty much how it happened. The Baby

Boomers turned forty, and things started to happen. One of the things that happened is that we started remembering what we forgot. We remembered how to bake bread; we remembered how to make cheese; we remembered how to make beer. "Specialty" was not born, but rediscovered. Many great business successes of this era have been by the companies that found the seams in between the megaliths. The giants were not always slain, but they did start sharing the stage with the specialists.

Walmart, founded in 1964, thrived, but so did companies such as the GAP, Banana Republic, and L.L. Bean. Kraft continued its march toward consolidation, but left in its wake the opportunities to be filled by the Ben & Jerrys, Stoneyfields, and Cabots of our time.

Initially, the demand was serviced by the specialty mail-order marketers, outgrowths of the Whole Earth Catalog. As demand grew, the market gravitated toward more traditional retail to service a broader demand.

Health, fitness, food, beer, spirituality—all of these areas were turned on their heads when the Boomers hit their strides in the 1980s. Whole Foods Markets were born. That, in turn, fueled much of the growth that Seventh Generation experienced for the cleaning products that they wholesale.

Nowhere is the evolution more evident than in beer. In the 1970s, Budweiser, Miller, and Coors (still a regional then) ruled the day. In 1978, home brewing was legalized—the first tiny fissure in the "wall" of the national brewers (who had successfully lobbied for the ban since the days of Prohibition). By the late '70s/early '80s, the first brewpubs and micros appeared, doing the groundwork for the success of Magic Hat and others in the '90s.

And, ultimately, the unthinkable happened in the beverage business: Budweiser was acquired by InBev in 2008. You might say that the "king of beers" became InBev's bitch. Like me, the Busch family was pushed out of their own business by the "money folks." The proud Coors family first merged with Molson, then Miller. This leaves the title of the largest American-owned, independent brewing company as a contest between Yuengling (founded in 1829) and Samuel Adams (founded in 1984)!

I'm ready to call this revolution over. We won!

So many of the companies that are today's success stories trace their origins to this period. Many have passed through their entrepreneurial stage and are either being bought out by private-equity companies (who have no clue how to operate a business or grow a brand, but are very good at making money or finding futures with new, multi-national partners). What's next for Baby Boomers?

Death, that's what.

I've been thinking a lot about death these days. Not "death" the reality, the inevitability, the eventuality, but "death" the business opportunity. Please allow me to introduce my current fantasy, Carpe Diem Industries.

As a marketing person, one thing I can state with absolute certainty. Over the next few decades, every single remaining Baby Boomer will die. Talk about a guaranteed growth opportunity! Here's another pearl of wisdom: we aren't going to be willing to die the same way our parents did. If we wouldn't accept their bread, their beer, and their ice cream, we're not going to accept their trip to the funeral home with the $5,000 velvet-lined coffin.

You can already see this in the way this generation is retiring. We're not!

Retirement in our parent's generation = gold watch, pension, Social Security, condo in Florida, death due to boredom. Retirement in our generation = iPhone, new venture, so-called security, mobile office.

Whoever figures out how this translates into actual products and behaviors is going to die a billionaire and will likely have figured out a way that you CAN take it with you. Will that success be in compostable coffins? How about solar-powered, digital tombstones with video panels that feature you telling your own life story in your own voice. Just hit the start button, and you'll see and hear: "Hi! This is Alan, coming to you live from the hereafter. Thanks for coming by to visit today. I was born in Brooklyn, New York, the son of second-generation Eastern European immigrants. My father was a real-estate developer, just back from a hitch in the Army . . . "

This could be big. Want to get in on the ground floor? This can't miss.

How do I know? I was born on November 10, 1946.

Are Entrepreneurs Nuts?

Afterword by Jerry Greenfield

In a word: yes. (All, except me, that is. I'm completely sane, the personification of a responsible and sober man. I guess that let's you know who is the real entrepreneurial genius in Ben & Jerry's.)

My dear friend and business partner, Ben Cohen, is a heck of a guy, but he's totally nutty, a certifiable lunatic. And I mean this in the best possible sense. Maybe "nuts" isn't the most precise word, but in my not-so-limited experience, those wacky folks who start their own ventures are a little different from the rest of us.

We all have ideas. It happens all the time. Ideas are the easy part. Some people have more than others; some people have better ideas than others. But most of us are smart enough not to do anything about our brilliant ideas until we've evaluated the idea in the clear light of dawn. Then, even if we think the idea is brilliant, we're smart enough not to quit the job or risk the life savings on an unproven venture.

But an entrepreneur just starts running. He or she doesn't think about it. They are spontaneous, impulsive, and intuitive. They are risk-takers and rule-breakers, utterly unafraid of failure. In their demented world they think of "failure" as an interesting learning experience. They feel no need for a business plan, no need to wait until things are in place and the time is right. They look forward to overcoming the obstacles that intimidate the rest of us. My partner Ben sometimes says that he'd rather fail at something new than succeed by following the proven path.

I speak at colleges a fair amount these days. There's definitely a trend in education to try to teach young people how to become entrepreneurs. While you can come up with a list of the principles and rules, I'm not sure that you can ever train someone to be an entrepreneur like you might train a lawyer, accountant, or doctor. Entrepreneurs learn more from experience than from books. They learn from their mistakes, and they learn to adapt to changing circumstances. The lucky ones eventually evolve into good and solid business people.

By this definition Alan Newman definitely qualifies as "nuts." Moreover, he's proved how nuts he is with different products in different industries. While it's tempting to focus on the more outrageous aspects of Alan's personality, it's important not to overlook what he is really good at. He's good at branding, but what does that mean? In my mind it means that he's good at creating a certain feeling around the product or service with which he's associated and able to communicate that feeling to others. That's the part of the business process that is labeled "marketing." Without wanting to sound too touchy-feely or New Age-y, what Alan is doing is expressing who he is on the inside to the rest of the world.

Entrepreneurs are always looking for a better way, a new experience, an opportunity. At the end of the day, they are the ones who move society, the culture, and even the species forward. The rest of us are grateful to be along for the ride. If that's "nuts," then please pass the bowl!

Jerry Greenfield is the "Jerry" of Ben & Jerry's.

Alan Newman is a most unlikely entrepreneur. You have to squint and read between the lines to see any indications that the person who lived the early and middle parts of his life would end up starting so many successful businesses.

Alan lives in Burlington, Vermont where he prospects for new business ventures, brainstorms with similarly afflicted friends and associates, and speaks to college students and trade associations about the joys and pitfalls of the entrepreneurial life.

To book Alan for a speaking engagement, email him at Alan@AlchemyandScience.com .

Promoting Free Speech Word-by-Word

The Public Press employs new technologies and the economics of scale -- "small" scale, that is -- to publish books that might not otherwise see the light of day. We then offer our titles a home so that they are accessible via traditional book trade channels.

The Public Press

We specialize in Author's Editions

For many, an Author's Edition will be the fastest and most reasonable route to publication. With our assistance the author manages pre-press operations, thereby achieving maximum control and financial opportunity at the lowest risk.

The Great Beer Trek (Replica edition)

This is an exact replica of the original published in 1984. It has been produced by The Public Press as a companion piece to the new edition that will be published in 2012. The Great Beer Trek chronicles a beer lover's quest to learn the "secret of the suds" in 1978, when Americans still thought of beer as a bland, fizzy, yellow beverage favored by blue collar slobs in their wife-beater undershirts. Author Morris saw beer and the beer drinker as more enlightened. In some circles the publication of this book is seen as one of the sparks that kindled what became a beer revolution. Now, with more than 1500 breweries (then, there were fewer than 50) and limitless varieties of brews to choose from, America has gone from a vast beer wasteland to one of sudsy meccas of the planet.

**$12.95 (plus $3.00 shipping and handling)
from The Public Press,
100 Gilead Brook Road, Randolph, VT 05060.
(802) 234.9101   ThePublicPress.com**

Stephen Morris's Vermont Trilogy

Beyond Yonder

When Darwin Hunter decides to update Over Yonder Hill (Alton Blanchard's history of the tiny Vermont hamlet of Upper Granville), the result is Beyond Yonder, a chronicle of the cultural divide between the entrenched natives and the invaders from the Land of Flat. From "Babysitters" to "Zucchinis" the contrasting world views are examined and skewered.

The King of Vermont

A chance comment on Vermont's most popular talk show, Straddlin' the Fence, lands Darwin Hunter in a three-way race to be elected State Senator. Set against a political landscape as rocky and muddy as the garden during Mud Season, Darwin combats his wily, experienced opponents with his only long suit–the truth.

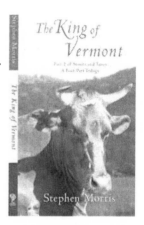

Stories & Tunes

The long-anticipated third volume of Morris's Vermont trilogy. Darwin Hunter is now the MegaBucks Czar, a man with unassailable authority over the state lottery. After an epiphany that reveals to him the regressive nature of this institutionalized gambling, Darwin becomes a modern day Robin Hood, using his power to more fairly distribute the wealth, at least in the Brigadoon that is Vermont.

**All titles by Stephen Morris $12.95
(plus $3 shipping and handling) from The Public Press,
100 Gilead Brook Road, Randolph, VT 05060
(802) 234.9101 ThePublicPress.com**

The Public Press

Author's Edition

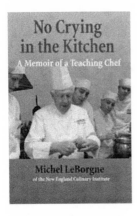

This author had a great story to tell, and a small but devoted audience, but needed more help with language and layout than a typical publisher could justify. The Public Press accommodated his needs easily and gracefully.

No Crying in the Kitchen
by Michel LeBorgne

This is the tasty story of Michel LeBorgne's journey through a culinary life, a life that started on a farm in Brittany and led eventually to the New England Culinary Institute. Michel learned the basics from master chefs in Paris. Like many other ambitious young men (Jacques Pepin comes to mind) Michel came to New York City and quickly found employment in some of the city's most fashionable restaurants. Eventually, however, Michel turned away from the grind of the restaurant life and took a job with Yale University's food service. For more than a decade he combined the flair of French cuisine with the needs of a massive institution. When the opportunity arose to take on the teaching chef duties at a start-up educational institute in Montpelier, Vermont, Michel jumped at the chance. Now chefs and restaurant owners worldwide have learned their kitchen skills at New England Culinary Institute, many under the watchful eye and guiding hand of Chef Michel LeBorgne.

**$21.95 (plus $3.00 shipping and handling)
from The Public Press,
100 Gilead Brook Road, Randolph, VT 05060.
(802) 234.9101   ThePublicPress.com**

I can't begin to imagine how many lives Chef Michel has touched over his expansive and celebrated cooking career. His wit, passion, and enthusiasm for all things is utterly infectious.

Alister Brown
Chef/Restaurateur, Wellington, New Zealand

Chef Michel's charming memoir can turn any cook with a sharp knife, a pinch of sea salt, and her grandmother's frying pan into a world class chef!

Ellen Michaud
author of A Master Class: Sensational Recipes from the Chefs of the New England Culinary Institute

I met Chef Michel more than 25 years ago when I first visited New England Culinary Institute as a young chef seeking externs for my very first kitchen brigade. I returned last year (2008) to address a graduating class and found Michel to be the same charming, energetic, and enthusiastic ambassador for NECI and his adopted home, Vermont.

Susan Spicer
Co-Founder, Bayona Restaurant, New Orleans, Louisiana

It takes a very special person to imagine how to develop a unique culinary training program, then plunge in as the jack of all trades on the first day. Michel's entertaining story highlights the many twists and turns of his childhood and his professional career that culminates with the establishment of New England Culinary Institute. It is a great read and revealing of the energy, will power and optimism that has helped Michel time and again to plunge ahead into the unknown.

Fran Voigt
Co-Founder New England Culinary Institute

This is great story of a great man. Thousands of young chefs in the US have been trained and mentored by Chef Michel, and admire and uphold his values. Definitely a spicy read for up and coming chefs, and for anyone who has a passion for product and a commitment to quality. Perfectly seasoned from a consummate professional.

Tom Bivins, NECI Class of '91
Executive Chef, New England Culinary Institute

℗ The Public Press

We specialize in
Community Supported Books (CSBs)

Some books have as their primary goal to support a specific community. Inspired by Community Supported Agriculture (CSAs) Community Supported Books can reach special interest markets that are not served by commercial publishers.

More books by Stephen Morris:
Stripah Love

While our hero (Artie) has achieved success, it's summarily withdrawn from him, arbitrarily, and unfairly. The lady of our tale, Shea, has achieved success, only to find that it exists in close proximity to the law of the jungle. Set on the muddy clam flats of Massachusetts Bay, this is a love story about fish and a fish story about love.

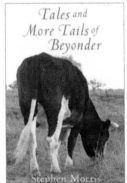

Tales (and More Tails) of Beyonder
Stephen Morris is an indefatigable chronicler of life in Beyonder, and this is his best work. This is a collection of his shorter pieces. His offerings on Mud Season and Vermont Holidays are particularly memorable.

**All titles by Stephen Morris $12.95
(plus $3 shipping and handling) from The Public Press,
100 Gilead Brook Road, Randolph, VT 05060
(802) 234.9101 ThePublicPress.com**